THE
NONPROFIT
PROBLEM
SOLVER

THE
NONPROFIT
PROBLEM
SOLVER

A MANAGEMENT GUIDE

RICHARD LORD

PRAEGER

New York
Westport, Connecticut
London

Library of Congress Cataloging-in-Publication Data

Lord, Richard.
    The nonprofit problem solver.

    Bibliography: p.
    Includes index.
    1. Corporations, Nonprofit—Management.   I. Title.
HD62.6.L67   1989   658'.048   88-32188
ISBN 0-275-93125-0 (alk. paper)

Library of Congress Catalog Card Number: 88-32188
ISBN: 0-275-93125-0

First published in 1989

Praeger Publishers, One Madison Avenue, New York, NY 10010
A division of Greenwood Press, Inc.

Printed in the United States of America

The paper used in this book complies with the
Permanent Paper Standard issued by the National
Information Standards Organization (Z39.48-1984).

10 9 8 7 6 5 4 3 2 1

CONTENTS

85620

THE
NONPROFIT
PROBLEM
SOLVER

1   WHAT ARE WE DOING HERE?

"It just fell into a crack."

We've all heard this excuse for why something didn't get done. Most of us have used it from time to time. Why wasn't the task completed? Either because nobody knew it needed to be done or because nobody accepted responsibility for doing it.

Nobody likes cracks. Things get lost in cracks. It takes a lot of work to pull them out. Somebody has to toil through the night to fix the mess. That person is the boss.

Life doesn't have to be so difficult. Cracks can be filled.

How? With people and with systems—but not just any people or any system. The right people have to be put in the right places and reminded when to do the right things. The first step to develop this system is to carefully analyze your organization's needs. Then you assign responsibility for each task and develop prenotification systems to remind the responsible employees of upcoming deadlines.

This is difficult in small organizations. People do many different jobs. The organizational style is informal, perhaps spontaneous. The organizations survive because they're blessed with employees who "pitch in" and do whatever is needed. This works well—up to a point. The work gets done because enthusiasm substitutes for efficiency. But, as the organization grows, problems become more complex. Toes get stepped on. Responsibility is never clearly assigned. People forget to file reports they previously completed instinctively.

A typical response to this dilemma is hiring more people. Fill the crack with bodies. The more staff members you have bumping into each other, the more likely it is that someone will remember what has to be done and that somebody will be available to do it.

There is another way to fill cracks. It's called management—the art of utilizing resources to their maximum. There must be a master plan in which all of the organization's work is assigned, tracing systems are created to ensure that deadlines are met, and all employees know what their role is and what other people should do.

This process has three components:

1. Identifying everything that must be done
2. Determining who is most capable of doing each task
3. Assigning responsibility to do each task

To switch from an informal organizational style to a managed organization requires analysis and planning. This chapter helps identify your organization's needs and develop a management plan.

WRITING JOB DESCRIPTIONS THAT WORK

Job descriptions can be straitjackets, or they can be the building blocks of an efficient organization, encouraging appropriate creativity. The way you design them makes the difference. How can you be sure that your job descriptions will help you achieve your organization's aims?

Use the building-blocks concept. Start by defining the tasks in your organization and placing them in logical clusters. Based on these clusters, develop an organizational chart and assign responsibilities to the available positions. Here's an example of how this can be done with a small museum.

The administrative work of the Hereford Museum consists of the tasks shown in Table 1.1. These tasks are analyzed using three criteria. They are described in terms of:

Table 1.1
Hereford Museum Administrative Tasks

TASK	TIME	SKILL*	LEVEL
paying bills	6 hours	cler	low
supervise professional & administrative staff	8 hours	super	high
meet with potential major donors	1 hour	mkt	high
collecting revenue	8 hours	cler	low
manage bank accounts	3 hours	fin	high
supervise maintenance of physical plant	4 hours	super	low
maintain insurance	1/4 hour	fin	high
do payroll	2 hours	fin	low
administer employee benefits	1 hour	cler	high
hire staff	1 hour	prog sup	high
type correspondence and reports	20 hours	cler	low
answer phone	6 hours	cler	high
answer door	4 hours	cler	low
receive, distribute and send mail	5 hours	cler	low
prepare financial reports	2 hours	fin	high
prepare tax returns	1 hour	fin	high
apply for grants	10 hours	mkt	high
purchase supplies	4 hours	cler	high
administer grants	3 hours	prog sup	high
administer program	10 hours	prog sup	high
execute annual giving campaign	13 hours	mkt	low
maintain program files	2 hours	cler	low
community relations	5 hours	mkt	high
maintain financial files	1 hour	cler	low
maintain correspond files	2 hours	cler	low

Table 1.1 (continued)

TASK	TIME	SKILL*	LEVEL
primary journal entries	10 hours	fin	low
General Ledger (GL) entries	6 hours	fin	high
manage bank accounts	3 hours	fin	high
develop & execute budget	6 hours	fin	high
professional relations	3 hours	prog sup	high
assure compliance with governmental regulations	1 hour	prog sup	high
develop and execute long range plan	2 hours	prog sup	high

* cler= clerical, super= administrative supervision, mkt= marketing, prog sup= prog supervision

1. The estimated amount of time that it takes to perform each task (tasks that are performed less than weekly are annualized and the total is divided by 52 to establish a weekly figure)
2. The type of skill involved
3. The skill level

The tasks are then clustered according to the type of skill required (Table 1.2). This involves developing separate professional departments, so time is added to each cluster for meeting with the CEO. The clusters can be placed in a diagram, as in Figure 1.1, showing any interrelations that may exist.

Following these lines, it's clear that the different clusters of tasks are highly interrelated. There are many ways the clusters can be combined to create specific jobs. For example, neither the program nor administrative supervisory functions are sufficient to support a full-time employee. So they will be joined into a single position. The task of meeting with major donors is then transferred from the marketing function to supervisory, so that each cluster has 35 hours of work per week (Table 1.3).

The clerical function is too much for one job, as it would require 59 hours per week. So we reassign to the financial function the 19 hours of weekly work that relates to business activities, such as paying

Table 1.2
Hereford Museum Administrative Tasks Skill Clusters

CLERICAL	HRS PER WEEK	SKILL LEVEL
paying bills	6 hours	low
maintain program files	2 hours	low
maintain financial files	1 hour	low
maintain correspond files	2 hours	low
collecting revenue	8 hours	low
type correspondence and reports	20 hours	low
answer phone	6 hours	high
answer door	4 hours	low
receive, distribute and send mail	5 hours	low
purchase supplies	4 hours	high
administer employee benefits	1 hour	high
TOTAL HOURS	59 hours	

FINANCIAL	HOURS PER WEEK	SKILL LEVEL
primary journal entries	10 hours	low
gl entries	6 hours	high
manage bank accounts	3 hours	high
maintain insurance	1/4 hour	high
prepare financial reports	2 hours	high
prepare tax returns	1 hour	high
develop & execute budget	6 hours	high
meet with Board	1 hour	high
meet with CEO	2 hours	high
do payroll	2 hours	low
TOTAL HOURS	33 1/4 hours	

Table 1.2 (continued)

PROGRAM SUPERVISION	HOURS PER WEEK	SKILL LEVEL
hire staff	1 hour	high
meet with Board	2 hours	high
administer program	10 hours	high
administer grants	3 hours	high
professional relations	3 hours	high
assure compliance with governmental regulations	1 hour	high
develop and execute long range plan	2 hours	high
TOTAL HOURS	22 hours	

ADMINISTRATIVE SUPERVISION	HOURS PER WEEK	SKILL LEVEL
supervise maintenance of physical plant	4 hours	low
Supervise administrative depts	8 hours	high
TOTAL HOURS	12 hours	

MARKETING	HOURS PER WEEK	SKILL LEVEL
apply for grants	10 hours	high
execute annual giving campaign	13 hours	low
community relations (lay)	5 hours	high
meet with CEO	2 hours	high
meet with potential major donors	1 hour	high
media relations	5 hours	high
TOTAL HOURS	36 hours	

Figure 1.1
Hereford Museum Cluster Relationships

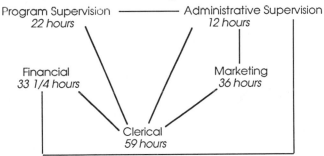

bills, maintaining financial files, collecting revenue, and purchasing supplies. The changes in these two areas are shown in Table 1.4.

All of the functions now fit neatly into 35- to 40-hour weekly packages, with the exception of the financial function, which is over 40 hours, but not sufficient for two full-time jobs. So the function is split, based on skill levels, to create one full-time function (Business Manager) and one part-time (Bookkeeper). The Business Manager is also given three hours per week for supervision of the Bookkeeper (Table 1.5). With these revised work loads, the organizational chart shown in Figure 1.2 is developed.

Now it's time to write job descriptions. Do this by combining specific tasks in sufficiently general descriptions to allow flexibility.

Job Description: CEO

Reports to: Board of Directors
Status*: Nonexempt
1. Recruits, hires, evaluates, and terminates professional and support staff
2. Informs the Board of Directors of the museum's operations; implements Board policies through the supervision of program and administrative departments
3. Ensures compliance with government regulations and administers grants

---

*Status defines whether an individual is exempt from wage and hour legislation. Nonprofessional employees are subject to these laws, and their work hours must be specified.

Table 1.3
Hereford Museum Reorganized Supervisory and Marketing Functions
SUPERVISORY

	HOURS PER WEEK	SKILL LEVEL
hire staff	1 hour	high
meet with Board	2 hours	high
administer program	10 hours	high
administer grants	3 hours	high
professional relations	3 hours	high
assure compliance with governmental regulations	1 hour	high
develop and execute long range plan	2 hours	high
supervise maintenance of physical plant	4 hours	low
supervise administrative depts	8 hours	high
meet with potential major donors	1 hour	high
TOTAL HOURS	35 hours	

MARKETING

	HOURS PER WEEK	SKILL LEVEL
apply for grants	10 hours	high
execute annual giving campaign	13 hours	low
community relations (lay)	5 hours	high
meet with CEO	2 hours	high
meet with potential major donors	1 hour	high
media relations	5 hours	high
TOTAL HOURS	35 hours	

Table 1.4
Hereford Museum Reorganized Clerical and Financial Functions

CLERICAL

	HOURS PER WEEK	SKILL LEVEL
maintain program files	2 hours	low
maintain correspond files	2 hours	low
type correspondence and reports	20 hours	low
answer phone	6 hours	high
answer door	4 hours	low
receive distribute and send mail	5 hours	low
administer employee benefits	1 hour	high
TOTAL HOURS	40 hours	

FINANCIAL

	HOURS PER WEEK	SKILL LEVEL
manage bank accounts	3 hours	high
maintain insurance	1/4 hour	high
prepare financial reports	2 hours	high
prepare tax returns	1 hour	high
develop & execute budget	6 hours	high
do payroll	2 hours	low
GL entries	6 hours	high
primary journal entries	10 hours	low
purchase supplies	4 hours	high
collecting revenue	8 hours	low
paying bills	6 hours	low
maintain financial files	1 hour	low
meet with CEO	2 hours	high
meet with Board	1 hour	high
TOTAL HOURS	52 1/4 hours	

Table 1.5
Hereford Museum Segregation of Business Manager and Bookkeeper Functions

BUSINESS MANAGER

	HOURS PER WEEK	SKILL LEVEL
purchase supplies	4 hours	high
gl entries	6 hours	high
meet with Board	1 hour	high
meet with CEO	2 hours	high
manage bank accounts	3 hours	high
maintain insurance	1/4 hour	high
prepare financial reports	2 hours	high
prepare tax returns	1 hour	high
develop & execute budget	6 hours	high
collecting revenue	8 hours	low
TOTAL HOURS	33 1/4 HOURS	

	HOURS PER WEEK	SKILL LEVEL
BOOKKEEPER		
primary journal entries	10 hours	low
maintain financial files	1 hour	low
paying bills	6 hours	low
TOTAL HOURS	17 HOURS	

Figure 1.2
Hereford Museum Organizational Chart

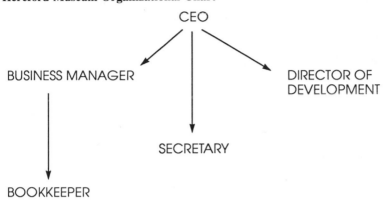

4. Represents the museum in professional organizations and meets with potential major donors
5. In consultation with the Board of Directors, assumes responsibility for all areas of operations, both financial and programmatic

Job Description: Business Manager

Reports to: CEO
Supervises: Bookkeeper, Secretary (for employee benefits)
Status: Exempt
1. Submits proposed annual budget to the Board of Directors and implements the budget approved by the Board
2. Prepares appropriate financial reports and tax returns. Maintains General Ledger
3. Manages museum's cash assets
4. Purchases supplies
5. Evaluates and reports to the Board regarding the adequacy of insurance coverage
6. Performs other duties and tasks as assigned by the CEO

Job Description: Director of Development

Reports to: CEO
Status: Exempt
1. Prepares corporate and foundation grant proposals

2. Plans and implements annual giving campaign

3. Informs the museum's constituency of developments within the museum to encourage their donations; informs the press of significant developments

4. Performs other duties and tasks as assigned by the CEO

Job Description: Secretary

Reports to: CEO
Status: Nonexempt
Hours: Monday–Friday, 9–5

1. Answers the phone and greets visitors, taking messages when necessary

2. Types correspondence and reports; receives, distributes, and sends mail; maintains correspondence and program files

3. At direction of Business Manager, administers employee benefit claims

4. Performs other duties and tasks as assigned by the CEO

Job Description: Bookkeeper

Reports to: Business Manager
Status: Nonexempt
Hours: Monday, Wednesday, Friday, 9–3

1. Makes primary journal entries

2. Issues checks for payment of invoices

3. Calculates and executes payroll

4. Maintains financial files

5. Performs other duties and tasks as assigned by Business Manager

This strategy works for an organization of any size. Larger organizations require more time to complete each task. So the building blocks (job descriptions) can be further limited in scope. Employees perform fewer functions and the tasks are more closely related in terms of type and level of skill. But remember to always maintain flexibility to ensure that the unexpected can be handled.

DON'T MISS THE DEADLINE

It seems to come out of nowhere. If you receive one, you certainly will wish that it would go back to that same nowhere it came from.

But it won't.

It's a notice of failure to submit required reports to government agencies.

Working your way through government bureaucracies to correct these errors is a nightmare. Few activities can consume more of your time while threatening your existence. The fines for noncompliance can be astronomical. The frustration of devoting countless hours to corresponding and talking with bureaucrats is immense.

Once you have been caught, there are few alternatives to gritting your teeth and complying with whatever is required. There are no shortcuts to getting yourself out of these problems. You are in serious trouble. It will take a long time to correct.

The solution to this problem is to avoid it. Ensure that you complete all reports when they are due. You probably do this already for all reports of which you are aware. The killers are those that you didn't know that you were required to complete.

Who requires reports from nonprofits? Many different government agencies from the federal level through to, in some cases, the local level. Some are required from all commercial enterprises, some from all tax-exempt organizations, some from real property owners, some from schools, and so on.

The most secure technique for ensuring that you are aware of all required reports is to ask your accountant for a written schedule of them. There is no way that you could anticipate all of the possible agencies that could require reports. Let your accountant take responsibility for having provided you with a complete list.

To get started, here's a description of the primary reports required by the Internal Revenue Service from nonprofits that have employees. As you read through this list, have a year calendar with large boxes to write in at your side. Note the type of report required in the box of relevant dates for the entire year. When you get the schedule from your accountant, do the same transferral of information to the calendar. Hang the calendar in a prominent place and refer to it often. You'll have a constant reminder of your reporting deadlines.

Every tax-exempt organization must file a Return of Organization Exempt from Income Tax (Form 990). Most service-providing nonprofits are nonprivate foundations and must attach schedule A to their form 990. This is the equivalent of an income tax return for nonprofits, in which you report your financial activity for the fiscal year. The form 990 must be filed four and a half months after the close of the fiscal year. This is May 15 for an organization that ends its fiscal year on December 31. For organizations that close their fiscal year on June 30, the deadline is November 15.

In addition, an organization that has over $1,000 of unrelated business income in a year must file an Exempt Organization Business Income Tax Return (form 990-T). To a certain extent, the definition of unrelated business income is open to interpretation, so you should request your accountant's opinion concerning whether this report applies to your organization. The basic concept is that unrelated business income is revenue that a nonprofit receives in return for providing a good or service other than the service, or related goods, for which the organization received its tax exemption. A community residence that has a restaurant and uses the profits to support the residence probably would be subject to unrelated business income tax. A school that sells academic supplies to its students probably would not be subject to unrelated business income tax. The form 990-T is due at the same time as the form 990—four and a half months after the close of the fiscal year.

Can't make the deadlines? No problem. Just file an "Application for Extension of Time to File" (form 2758) on or before the due date for the form 990, schedule A, or form 990-T. You can receive an extension of up to two months.

When a person is hired or an employee's federal income tax withholding allowances change, that person must complete an Employee's Withholding Allowance Certificate (form W-4). This provides the basis for determining the number of allowances for payroll taxes. Accept no substitutes, such as oral information or a memo. These forms must be kept on file permanently. If an employee elects more than ten allowances or claims exemption from tax and earns over $200 per week, you must send a copy of the W-4 to the IRS.

Within three days of beginning work, all new employees must complete an Employment Eligibility Verification Form (form I-9) and submit it to you with either proof of American citizenship or authorization for an alien to work in the United States. You record the information concerning the proof of citizenship or alien work authorization and maintain the I-9 on file for three years. This is not an IRS requirement—it comes from the Immigration and Naturalization Service, so get the forms from the INS.

Tax Deposit Forms (form 8109) accompany your payroll tax withholding deposits. Deposits must be made with an authorized financial institution (probably your bank) at any time that you are holding the following combined amounts of federal income tax, FICA withheld from employees, and the employer's share of FICA:

—over $3000: within three banking days

—between $500 and $3000: fifteenth day of the following month

—under $500: with your quarterly report (see below)

Quarterly Return of Withheld Tax (form 941) is filed on the last day of the month following each quarter. Due dates are January 31, April 30, July 31, and October 31. This form is the final calculation of the taxes withheld and serves as a record of your tax deposits.

A Wage and Tax Statement (form W-2) reports an employee's actual earnings and taxes withheld for the preceding calendar year. These are due to the employee by January 31. Copies of all W-2s are due to the IRS by February 28, accompanied by a Transmittal of Income and Tax Statements (form W-3).

Any individual who received over $600 in a year from your organization and was not issued a form W-2 must receive a Miscellaneous Income report (form 1099). This includes payments to consultants and other independent contractors, who do not have Employer Identification Numbers, as well as private lenders to whom you pay interest. The deadlines for this are the same as the W-2—January 31 to the individual and February 28 to the IRS. The transmittal form for the 1099s is the form 1096. It is due to the IRS by February 28.

As mentioned before, this is not a complete list of all required reports. The complete list is specific to your organization, based on the scope of your operations and where you're located. Ask your accountant to identify other required reports.

A word of caution: Retain in your files copies of all reports you submit. Send all reports that you mail to any government authority by certified mail. If they don't receive it, you have proof that you're not at fault.

2 HAPPINESS IS A POSITIVE CASH FLOW

What is the most outstanding attribute of the nonprofit manager? Is it altruism? Dedication? Optimism? It's all of these—plus one overlooked characteristic: the grey hairs caused by worrying about how to get through the next payroll.

It's a depressing scenario. Many nonprofit managers report their greatest frustration is "putting out fires" that never get resolved—especially cash-flow problems. This is because the solutions they implement are short-term answers. The most common response is to view the impending doom as a fund-raising opportunity. Beg Board members and wealthy benefactors for a transfusion of cash to keep the organization afloat.

This strategy may be successful a few times, but eventually donors see it as a sign of poor management. Each time you go back to them, they're less likely to give you the help you need.

The long-term solution is effective cash-flow management. This strategy encourages your supporters to give you more over time. They don't want to have to pull you out of a crisis. Donors want to be associated with a winner. In addition to strengthening your fund-raising base, effective cash-flow management will:

1. Increase revenue—you'll receive more interest income
2. Decrease expenses—you'll borrow more efficiently

As a result, you'll be able to provide more services without increasing fees or donations.

How do you do it? By eliminating the causes for shortfalls. The most common roadblocks to effective cash management are failures to:

1. Collect money due to your organization on time
2. Use commercial credit effectively
3. Borrow cash efficiently

The corollary to this is that, if you collect receipts promptly, use credit effectively, and borrow efficiently you'll have fewer cash-flow problems. And you will grow fewer grey hairs.

The materials that follow provide techniques to overcome cash-flow roadblocks. Use these procedures and your cash will start to flow more smoothly.

FROM DEADBEATS TO DEADLINES—EFFECTIVE COLLECTION PROCEDURES

Collecting bills—it's probably the most unpleasant task that faces nonprofit managers. It's very upsetting to chase deadbeats. Just when you think you've heard every excuse, someone will come up with a new reason for why they haven't paid you. It's especially maddening when vendors start curtailing your credit because you can't pay them.

There is no magic solution that will make this problem vanish completely. But there are techniques you can use that will reduce the frequency of slow payment and default. Follow these procedures and you'll be able to spend more time on pleasant tasks. Effective collection procedures are built upon a three-step strategy.

The first step is to develop a clear timetable for debt collection. Don't wait until you have a problem to act. It will be ready when you need it. And be consistent in enforcing it.

Next, keep your fee-payers apprised of the status of their accounts. Make sure that they are aware of your expectations for payment.

Finally, respond quickly and firmly when a fee-payer doesn't meet a deadline.

Figure 2.1
Timetable for Debt Collection

DAY	ACT	NOTES
1	1.Commitment for debt secured	
	2. Service provided	
	3. Payment required per commitment	
	4. Statement issued	
	5. Past due statement issued	
	6. Past due letter	
	7. Past due call by staff	
	8. Past due call by Director	
	9. Terminate services	

Before implementing your strategy, get it approved by your Board. Some people will get angry when you start insisting on payment—make sure you have your Board's support before you do it.

To formulate your strategy, complete the timetable for debt collection (Figure 2.1). In the left column, write the number of days (from the beginning of the process) that will pass before you perform each of the tasks. For example, if you decide to do the second step eight days after the first, and the third step six days after the second, put "8" to the left of Step 2 and "14" to the left of Step 3. In the right column, write any explanatory notes. For example, next to Step 1, you might write "tuition contract" if this is the form of debt security you use. Detailed explanations of each step follow. They'll help you determine when and how to perform the required tasks.

TIMETABLE FOR DEBT COLLECTION: EXPLANATORY NOTES

1. *Commitment for Debt Secured*

Before you permit someone to begin receiving services, make sure that they (or a person responsible for them) has signed a contract to pay. The following information should be specified in the contract:

1. The type of services to be provided
2. The dates of service
3. The amount to be paid
4. The payment schedule
5. The conditions under which a full or partial refund or cancellation of debt will be granted

After the fee-payer has signed the contract, have an officer of your corporation countersign it.

It's a good idea to have your lawyer review the contract before you start using it. The following draft can serve as a starting point.

Draft Commitment

I, the undersigned, *(name)* hereby enroll in the Upside Down Juggling Center for the class session during the period *(date)–(date)*.

The total tuition charge for the session is *(amount)*. This includes instructional fees for the School's basic program and materials and supplies provided by teachers. Additional charges may be incurred for special activities and breakage.

Tuition is to be paid in three installments. A nonrefundable deposit of *(amount)* is due on *(date)*. Sixty percent of *(amount)* is due on *(date)*. The remaining balance *(amount)*, is due on *(date)*.

Should Upside Down Juggling Center request that my enrollment be terminated before the completion of the contract term, a prorated refund of tuition will be made for the balance of the class session.

Agreed to:

For the school: _____

Title: _____   Date: _____

Student's signature: _____   Date: _____

2. *Service Provided*

You can't collect payment for a service unless you provide it. Regardless of the protections you build into a contract, you'll have a hard time getting money from a person who never appeared to receive your service.

One way to reduce your losses from no-shows is by requiring a nonrefundable deposit. You can keep this, even if the person never attends your program. The purpose of the deposit is to hold the space for the individual. If he or she does not use that space, you are the damaged party (in the eyes of the law) since you suffered a loss of revenue. So you can keep the deposit as restitution for this loss.

3. *Payment Required per Commitment*

From this day, start counting the days of delinquency to determine when you implement collection actions.

Routine Collection

4. *Statement Issued*

Statements should be sent at a routine time every month. If they're issued sporadically, people will become confused.

Send a statement to any account that had a charge or made a payment during the period as well as any that had a balance due at the beginning of the period (see Figure 2.2). The following information should appear on every statement:

Header Information

1. Your organization's name and address
2. Date of statement
3. Name and address of person responsible for the account
4. Name of the person receiving services, if he or she is different from the person responsible for account
5. The cut-off date for recording charges and payments on the statement, if it is different from the statement date. Include the notation, "This statement reflects charges and payments received through (date)."

Activity Information

1. Start by noting any balance due. This entry should include
    (a) Opening date of the previous statement period as the date of charge. For example, if this is the February 1 statement and the individual had an outstanding balance on the January 1 statement, the date of charge would be January 1.
    (b) Description of the charge should be BALANCE FORWARD.
    (c) Amount of balance due.
2. Next, enter the charges and payments that occurred during the period. Include:
    (a) The date the charge was incurred or the payment was received
    (b) A description of the activity. For payments, it should be "Payment received." For charges, be specific; don't just say "Tuition." Say "Tuition for fall semester, 19____."
    (c) Amount of the payment or charge.
3. Balance due. If it is a credit balance, it should be noted as such.

Figure 2.2
Sample Statement Form

Date: 4/3/8X

UPSIDE DOWN JUGGLING CENTER
110 Star Lane
Ketchum, Idaho

TO: Yogi Fourhands
872 Pin Road
Moonville, Idaho

STATEMENT OF ACCOUNT THROUGH 4/1/8X

DATE	DESCRIPTION	AMOUNT
3/1	Balance Forward	16.89
3/17	Payment received	-10.00
3/24	Breakage	32.00
Balance Due		38.89

Outstanding Balance due upon receipt

4. Terms of payment. Specify—is payment due upon receipt, within 10 days, when?

Slow Payment Techniques

5. *Past Due Statement*

Send past due statements to all clients who have outstanding balances. Do this as part of your regular statement cycle. You can use the same form as for the regular statements. The only differences are that it shows only the past due balance forward, and the terms should include a notification that the account is in arrears.

6. *Past Due Letter*

If the person still doesn't pay, it's time for personalized correspondence. The letter should follow the past due statement after a predetermined period of time, such as two weeks. Type or word-process this letter. Don't send a photocopied form letter. You want the delinquent to think that no one else is getting the same letter. Don't let the person think that there might be strength in numbers. Here's a sample.

Sample Past Due Letter

Dear Mr. Fourhands:

Your account at Upside-Down Juggling Center is considerably past due.

Please remit the arrears of *(amount)*. If you cannot pay the full outstanding balance at this time, please contact the Business Office.

We look forward to your prompt payment.

Sincerely,

Director

Personal Contact

7. *Staff Call*

As the process continues, the communications become more personal. The next step is for a staff member, usually the Business Manager, to call. Do this no more than two weeks after the letter from the Director. By quickening the pace between communications, you're making it clear that the matter is not being forgotten.

The aim of the call is to get a specific commitment as to when the account will be paid. Your tone should be firm but nonthreatening. Open with, "Your account is X weeks overdue and you haven't responded to the bills and letters that we've sent you. I am calling to see when we can expect payment."

Most likely, the person will try to get off the hook with an evasive answer, such as, "Within the next six months."

If you accept that, you've lost. Don't let the debtor off the phone until you've achieved your goal. You have to get a commitment that payment will be made by a specific date that is in the clearly foreseeable future. Your firmness may be answered with a "hard times song."

Respond by becoming a bureaucrat. Refer to policy and remove yourself from the decision. Fall back upon: "That is unacceptable according to our policies."

Don't let the debtor think that you have the power to make a decision. Present your demand as a hard reality. Switch the emphasis from the person's problems to developing a payment plan.

8. *Director Call*

If the person misses the payment deadline you established in the staff call, follow immediately with a call from the Director or a Board member.

End the call with the explicit threat that if payment is not received by a specified date, services will be terminated. Sometimes this works; sometimes it doesn't. Business Managers often are the toughest on deadbeats. Directors and Trustees tend to be very sympathetic.

Even if the call doesn't bring payment, it is a very important step. You're involving a superior in the decision to terminate services. Denying services to someone is unpleasant. Let a higher-up see the futility of dealing with this deadest of deadbeats. You'll have their support when the going gets tough.

Final Actions

9. *Terminate Services*

If the individual does not make an acceptable commitment to pay as the result of the call from the Director or fails to pay on the agreed date, follow immediately with a certified letter, return receipt requested. In this letter, notify the individual of the date on which services will be terminated if they do not pay.

Allow the individual two to three weeks to receive the letter and for you to receive the return receipt. A letter sent on the first of the month should specify that the last service date will be between the fifteenth and the twenty-second.

Now what? Turn the case over to a pro—either to a debt collection service or a lawyer. Often a debt collector has a higher chance of success. They'll put the time into the case that it requires. Unless the amount owed is considerable, lawyers usually are unenthusiastic. They won't be able to get enough of a fee from the collection to make it worth their time. Don't be too optimistic about the chances of collecting after an individual has left your program. But, by following the preceding plan, you probably won't have to use these sources of last resort very often.

MOTIVES FOR HOLDING CASH

Once you have your collection techniques working efficiently, you're ready to move on to the second phase of cash flow management—control of disbursements and management of short-term investments. How long do you hold the cash that you receive? When should you pay your bills? And what should you do with temporary cash surpluses?

The guiding principle used to answer these questions is the "time value" of money. Over time, money you hold can grow with additional revenue from interest earnings. The opposite is also true. When you owe money, it can cost you interest.

Efficient cash management maximizes net interest gain. This is measured as interest earned less interest paid. It's a step beyond just having enough money to pay your bills. It is the manipulation of debt and interest-earning opportunities to generate additional revenue. Cash management is more than merely having funds available to pay expenses when they fall due—it is using your funds to make money.

Commercial cash management presents many opportunities for creating interest income. There are many techniques utilized by vendors and banks that aren't called "savings" or "loans." They have different names, like "discounts" and "compensating balances." It isn't obvious, at first glance, but these options represent opportunities that can affect your interest income.

The key to cash management is evaluating the form in which you hold funds and how long you hold them before disbursement. The criteria for determining the efficiency of these operations is called the "opportunity cost." What this means is, if you don't use the money for the purpose you're intending, what else could you do with it? What opportunities for using the funds are you eliminating by using them in the way that you are using them? If you were to delay payment of a bill, what would it cost you? What would you gain? If you were to pay it sooner than you had scheduled, what would it cost you? What would you gain?

The point of this analysis is to ensure that you are receiving the highest possible interest revenue. Be greedy. Don't settle for merely earning interest—get the most revenue possible. This can be accomplished only by knowing what your options are and choosing the most profitable one.

The first process to analyze is your schedule for payment to vendors. A significant portion of your operating budget is probably spent on goods and services that are provided by vendors on credit. Unless otherwise specified, they expect to be paid 30 days from the date of their invoice. Take advantage of the 30-day grace period. Follow the basic rule of holding your cash in an interest-generating form, such as a money market account, as long as possible. The effect could be dynamic.

To see how this works, let's look at what happens if you pay your bills upon receipt. There is probably an average ten-day lag between the date the invoice is issued and it arrives on your desk, ready for payment. This delay creates an opportunity for generating some interest, if you hold your funds in an interest-generating form. Let's say that you spend $200,000 per year with vendors who provide credit and that your money market account pays 6 percent annual interest. The lag between the issuance date of the invoice and when you pay it can result in interest earnings of:

$$\frac{10 \text{ day delay}}{365 \text{ days per year}} \times \quad \$200{,}000 \text{ annual invoices} \times .06 \text{ interest rate}$$

$$= \$328.77 \text{ interest earned}$$

But the practice of paying upon receipt as opposed to 30 days from invoice date is costing you $657. That is the amount of interest to which you're entitled, but you are forfeiting by paying so promptly. If you pay after 30 days, the above calculation becomes:

$$\frac{30}{365} \times \$200{,}000 \times .06 = \$986.31$$

The difference is $986 − $329 = $657. That is the opportunity cost of paying upon receipt. It is revenue to which you are entitled that you are forfeiting.

It's hard to think of an economic justification for paying an invoice before it's due. Nevertheless, there are times that it is worth it to pay quickly. Some vendors have caught on to this game and offer incentives for paying sooner. These incentives are called "discounts." They reduce the amount that you owe when you pay promptly. For example, the cost of the goods you ordered was $1,000. But the invoice has a notation that if you pay within ten days, you need to pay only $990. Sounds like a good deal, but is it worth it?

To determine the relative value of a discount, compare the savings offered with other opportunities that are available to you for using the same money in another way. If the amount that you save by taking advantage of the discount is more than you could earn by keeping the money in an interest-generating form, the discount is worth it. If the opposite were true and the amount that you could earn in interest for the same money were more than the savings offered by the discount, the payment should be delayed.

Price discounts usually are expressed in dollar amounts, so you need to calculate the interest rate that the discount represents to make the comparison. Using the above example, a $1,000 invoice arrives with a notation that if it is paid within 10 days, the cost is reduced to $990. To determine whether this is worth it, perform the following calculation:

$$\frac{\text{amount of discount}}{\text{discounted amount}} \times \frac{365 \text{ (days in a year)}}{30\text{—number of days within which payment is required to qualify for discount}} = \text{annual interest rate}$$

In the above example, this would work out to:

$$\frac{10}{990} \times \frac{365}{20} = 18.43\%$$

If you have investment opportunities that pay more than 18.43 percent, you shouldn't prepay. However, if a 6 percent money market is where your money is sitting, you will make money by using the discount option.

It goes even further. If you don't have the cash available to prepay, it might make sense to delay paying an overdue bill and incur the finance charge. If you could "borrow" the $990 for three weeks with a finance charge of 12 percent, it would be worthwhile. You would actually be making 6.43 percent interest.

Another area to consider in your cash-flow management is payroll. For service-providing nonprofits, personnel costs often are the largest part of their budget. The timing of payroll can be powerful in determining interest earnings.

Let's say you have a payroll of $520,000 per year and you pay your employees weekly. Your weekly payroll is $10,000. By switching to a system in which you pay your employees every other week, you could hold $10,000 for an additional week 26 times per year. Assuming a 6 percent interest rate, you end up with:

$$\frac{26 \text{ weeks}}{52 \text{ weeks}} \times .06 \text{ interest rate} \times 10,000 = \quad \$300 \text{ additional interest income}$$

An added advantage to paying less often is that you'll reduce the bookkeeping costs. Extending the period between paychecks from one to two weeks, you reduce the number of payroll checks that you write by 50 percent. You'll cut your payroll bookkeeping in half. The savings from this probably will be even greater than the additional interest income.

Another way to improve cash management is by manipulating bank charges to your advantage. There are two common types of charges that banks make to commercial clients—deficiency fees and service charges. Don't accept them as necessary evils. There are techniques you can use that will reduce their impact.

Banks use these fees and charges to obtain interest-free loans from customers. If your balance in non-interest-bearing accounts falls below a certain level, you are assessed a charge. If your balance is above that point, you are forgiven the charges. But, by meeting the balance requirements, you also are foregoing interest on the funds. The crucial issue is to determine how your net interest expense (viewing the fees and charges as a type of interest expense) will be affected by keeping the funds in a non-interest-bearing account.

A compensating balance often is required by a bank that has lent money to an organization. If the average daily balance in non-interest-

bearing accounts falls below a specified level, the institution is charged a deficiency fee. The rate of interest usually is the same as the loan.
  It works like this:

$100,000   compensating balance level
−$70,000   average daily balance (annual)
$30,000
×0.10   agreed interest rate
$3,000   deficiency fee (annual)

Meet the compensating balance requirement if you don't have an opportunity to receive a higher rate of return on your funds than the rate that bank is using to calculate your deficiency fee. But if your interest-generating opportunities have a return of less than 10 percent, you'll make money by maintaining the compensating balance. In this case, if you have an opportunity to earn more than 10 percent interest on funds, maintain a minimal balance in your non-interest-bearing accounts.

Another type of compensating balance requirement is that which is required for discounted, or free, banking services. Many banks have a policy that if you keep a certain minimum balance in non-interest-bearing accounts, you will not be assessed bank service charges. The relative value of these discounts is not obvious. Close scrutiny is required to determine whether you should be keeping your balance above the required level.

Let's say that you can invest your funds at a 9 percent rate of return. The bank requires a $2,500 average daily balance for free services. The opportunity cost of keeping $2,500 in a non-interest-bearing account is $.09 \times \$2,500 = \$215$. If your bank charges are over $215 per year, it's worth it for you to keep the $2,500 in a non-interest-bearing account. If they're less than $215, take advantage of your 9 percent investment opportunity.

Most cash management energy is directed toward gaining interest. The focus is on keeping the minimum amount possible in non-interest-bearing accounts. But these two practices—compensating balances and discounted bank charges—can make it worthwhile to keep funds in a non-interest-bearing account. Remember, the aim of cash management is to maximize net interest earnings. So concentrating solely upon gross interest earnings can be counterproductive. Bank charges and deficiency fees could cost more than the interest you earn. Effective cash management analyzes the cost of earning interest, not just the amount of interest received.

Regardless of how poor your organization is, there are times that it will have excess cash. What do you do with it? Keep it in the checking account? Put it in a savings account? What about a money market account? Are you fully responding to the surpluses as opportunities to generate revenue? The efficient movement of temporary cash surpluses between different types of accounts can increase interest revenue. How you keep money that isn't needed for immediate expenses is an important element of cash management.

There is a progression of devices for holding cash. The first stopping point for money you receive is your checking account. You don't receive interest for funds held here, but you have immediate access to them. The next step is an interest-bearing demand account, such as a money market. You earn interest, but there are restrictions on how often you can take money out of this type of account. These restrictions are called transaction costs, which are charges that the bank makes to you for moving your money from the money market. How much you should be holding in a money market account is determined by comparing the interest rate that you earn with the transaction costs of moving the money.

Often a bank will allow a certain number of transfers out of the money market at no charge. But you have to pay for excess withdrawals. In an efficient cash management system, how often you move money is determined by comparing the interest earnings to the transaction charge.

Let's look at the simple cash flow of a grant. Guiding Light has received a $100,000 grant to provide services over a six-month period. The budget and payment schedule is shown in Table 2.1. Over a four-week period, Guiding Light's cash needs are as shown in Table 2.2. The bank allows one free transfer every four weeks. Additional transfers cost $1 each. The money market account is paying 6 percent interest. To avoid bank charges, Guiding Light could transfer $15,540 at the start of each month. But that is not the most efficient cash management system. It is losing more interest income than it is saving on bank charges.

Table 2.1
Guiding Light Grant Budget

Item	Total Grant Amount	Payment Schedule
net salaries	$50,000	paid weekly
tax withholding and employer FICA	$20,000	paid alternate weeks
rent	$12,000	paid monthly
utilities	$3,000	paid monthly
office supplies & misc. expense	$5,000	paid weekly
consultants	$10,000	paid weekly
TOTAL	$100,000	

To determine when transfers should occur, calculate the interest earned per day in the money market and compare it with the transaction charge. Start by determining the daily interest rate:

$$\frac{\text{annual interest rate}}{365 \text{ (days in a year)}} = \text{daily interest rate}$$

At 6 percent annual interest, this equals

$$\frac{.06}{365} = .000164$$

Now determine the break-even point. At what point is the interest that you earn more than the bank charge for a transfer? The answer is given with the dollar/day formula:

$$\frac{\text{transaction cost}}{\text{daily interest rate}} = \text{dollar/day}$$

In Guiding Light's case, this is

$$\frac{\$1.00}{\$0.000167} = \$6,000$$

Table 2.2
Guiding Light Weekly Cash Flow

WEEK ONE	net salaries	$\dfrac{50,000}{26}$	=	1920
	rent $\dfrac{12,000}{6}$		=	2000
	office supplies	$\dfrac{5000}{26}$	=	190
	consultants	$\dfrac{10,000}{26}$	=	380
TOTAL				4490
WEEK TWO	net salaries			1920
	withholding $\dfrac{20,000}{13}$		=	1540
	office supplies			190
	consultants			380
TOTAL				4030
WEEK THREE	net salaries			1920
	office supplies			190
	consultants			380
TOTAL				2490
WEEK FOUR	net salaries			1920
	withholding			1540
	office supplies			190
	consultants			380
	utilities $\dfrac{3000}{6}$		=	500
TOTAL				4530

If more than $6,000 can be held in the money market for one day, you'll make money by holding it in the money market. The interest earnings will be greater than the transaction cost. And the longer that you can hold the funds, the less you need to hold to offset the trans-

Table 2.3
Break-even Amounts for $6000/Day

Number of days	Calculation		Break-even amount
1	$6000/1	=	$6000
2	$6000/2	=	$3000
3	$6000/3	=	$2000
4	$6000/4	=	$1500
5	$6000/5	=	$1200
6	$6000/6	=	$1000
7	$6000/7	=	$857

action cost. For example, if you can hold $3,000 for two days, the results are the same as keeping $6,000 for one day. The amount that you need to hold for a specified period of time is determined by dividing the dollar/day figure by the number of days. See Table 2.3 for an example with $6,000 dollar/day. With this dollar/day formula, it's worth it to hold $890 for one week in the money market. The interest earned will be more than the transaction cost for the additional withdrawal. In Guiding Light's case, all weeks show over $890 in cash needs. It's worth it to make weekly transfers and incur the additional fees. The interest gain is shown in Table 2.4. Over the six-month life of the grant, this represents $140 of additional interest income.

The dollar/day formula also determines when to invest funds in the interest-generating account. An organization that receives large sums of money in advance of incurring expenses, such as Guiding Light, doesn't have a problem in this area. It places the funds, or a considerable portion of them, in an interest-bearing account, upon receipt. But the process is more complex for an organization that has a less

Table 2.4
Guiding Light Interest Gain Calculation

WEEK	CASH NEEDS	X	EXTRA DAYS HELD	X	DAILY INTEREST RATE	=	INTEREST GAIN
2	$4030		7		.000167		$4.71
3	$2490		14		.000167		$5.83
4	$4530		21		.000167		$15.90
					sub-total		$26.44
		less additional transaction costs ($1.00 x 3)					-$3.00
		net interest earnings (monthly)					$23.44

predictable inflow of cash. It can find itself at times with an excess of cash on hand. It needs to decide where to hold the surplus.

The first step is to plot your expense needs. We'll use the schedule that was presented for Guiding Light, in Table 2.5. The dollar/day factor, at 6 percent interest, is $6,000. On a weekly schedule this means that the interest gains will be greater than the transaction cost when the amounts shown in Table 2.6 are left in the interest-bearing account. This means that if there is $6,000 in excess cash in your account on the day before you need to make a withdrawal, you should transfer the $6,000 to the money market account. Just holding it over-night and taking it out the next day, you'll make more in interest than the $1.00 withdrawal charge. If there is $875 or more a week before a withdrawal is required, move it to the money market. Add to this your cash needs for the upcoming week, and the schedule in Table 2.7 appears.

At most points in this schedule the minimal amount required to be-gin making deposits in the non-interest-bearing account is the dollar/day for the particular day. For example, if you have $1,100 in the checking account on the second day, you should move it to the money market. All subsequent receipts for the week should also go to the money market. The only exception occurs near the withdrawal day. On the day before the withdrawal keep the amount of the withdrawal plus the dollar/day for the upcoming week in the checking account. In this case it would be the dollar/day for 8 days ($6,000/8 = 750$) plus the next day's withdrawal need: $750 + $4490 = $5240. On the day of the withdrawal start the cycle for the next week. If you have at least $875 left in the checking account after disbursing, move it to the money market.

The money market account is the first resting place for cash after the checking account. There are short-term investment instruments that

Table 2.5
Guiding Light Weekly Cash Needs

WEEK	EXPENSES
1	$4490
2	$4130
3	$2490
4	$4530

Table 2.6
Six Percent Interest-bearing Account Minimum Balances

DAY	AMOUNT
Withdrawal day (WD)	not applicable
WD - 1	$6000
WD - 2	$3000
WD - 3	$2000
WD - 4	$1500
WD - 5	$1200
WD - 6	$1000
WD - 7	$875

pay a higher return than a money market account. But every increase in interest earnings is accompanied by additional restrictions and/or risk. There's a tradeoff. The more restricted your access to the cash, the more you'll earn. If you're willing to go into higher risk, such as stocks and bonds, you can make more. However, the riskier ventures should not be entered into except by a qualified investments counselor. In this discussion we'll limit ourselves to the virtually risk-free instruments available through banks.

The next step up is certificates of deposit (CDs) and U.S. Government Treasury Bonds (T-Bills). Both are available through banks. They have a very low risk factor and their yield is higher than a money

Table 2.7
Six Percent Interest-bearing Account Deposit Schedule

DAY	WITHDRAWAL	$/DAY NEED	WEEK'S INITIAL M.M. DEPOSIT
8	4490	875	875
7	0	6000	5240
6	0	3000	3000
5	0	2000	2000
4	0	1500	1500
3	0	1200	1200
2	0	1000	1000
1	0	875	875

market account, but the cost of a premature redemption can be prohibitive.

CDs and T-Bills are available only in pre-established amounts, such as $5,000, $10,000 and so on. They are much more restrictive than money market accounts—the length and amount of deposit are rigid. You don't have the freedom to use them for whatever amount for whatever time you want, as you do with a money market. They are useful only for large amounts that you won't have to touch before the maturity date.

These investment instruments are usually offered in 30-day, 60-day, 90-day, six-month, one-year, and multi-year maturities. The longer the term of investment, the higher the interest rate. A 30-day term will have a yield virtually indistinguishable from a money market, a 60-day term will pay about 5 percent more than the money market rate, a 90-day about 10 percent more, and a six-month about 20 percent more. When a money market is paying 6 percent, a 60-day CD or T-Bill probably will pay approximately 6.3 percent, a 90-day will pay 6.6 percent, and a six-month investment will bring 7.2 percent.

Start developing your strategy by determining when you will use the funds. The schedule in Table 2.8 is for Guiding Light. As the interest rate on CDs and T-Bills increases with the length of the investment, search for the opportunity for the longest maturity. In this case the longest possible is three months, as the last of the funds must be available on the first day of the sixth month. Buy a $50,000 90-day CD or T-Bill when the $100,000 is first received. It will be redeemed on the first day of the fourth month.

The combined remaining balances in the money market and check-

Table 2.8
Guiding Light Monthly Money Market Balance Schedule

Month	Beginning of month money market balance	Month's cash needs
1	100,000	17,000
2	83,000	16,500
3	66,500	16,500
4	50,000	17,000
5	33,000	16,500
6	16,500	16,500

Table 2.9
Guiding Light Initial Investment Schedule

Month	Available for investment	Month's cash needs
1	50,000	17,000
2	33,000	16,500
3	16,500	16,500
4	50,000*	17,000
5	33,000	16,500
6	16,500	16,500

*CD/T-Bill redeemed

ing accounts are still available for investment. The amounts are as in Table 2.9. Now we start looking for 60-day investment opportunities. Two appear. A $15,000 instrument can be bought on the first day of the month with a maturity date of the first day of the third month. Another $15,000 can be bought on the first day of the fourth month to be redeemed on the first day of the sixth month. This leaves money market checking balances as listed in Table 2.10.

Virtually every organization has the potential to generate interest income by holding excess cash effectively. How you hold these tem-

Table 2.10
Guiding Light Final Investment Schedule

Month	Money market/checking balance (First of month)	Month's cash needs
1	35,000	17,000
2	18,000	16,500
3	16,500*	16,500
4	35,000**	17,000
5	18,000	16,500
6	16,500	16,500

* $1500 remaining on the first of the month plus proceeds of redemption of $15,000 CD or T-Bill
** proceeds of redemption of $50,000 CD or T-Bill less $15,000 invested in 60 day CD or T-Bill

porary surpluses is an important element of cash-flow management. The first step in taking advantage of these possibilities to increase revenue is to recognize the opportunities when they occur. Then determine if the amount of interest you receive less the transaction costs will create a gain. You'll probably find that merely by moving funds between accounts at the appropriate times you will increase your organization's revenue. And you'll have the satisfaction of utilizing one of your organization's resources to its fullest.

HOW TO BORROW

Tomorrow is payday. You don't have the money in the bank to cover the payroll. But you're not worried. Last week you applied for a loan. You call the bank to make sure everything is going on schedule. The banker tells you:

Mr. Whetherbee, there's a delay with your application. The people in our credit department want more information concerning your revenue. They need copies of your contracts with the state. If you get them to me today, we might be able to get the loan through by the end of next week.

I'm sorry about this delay, but they just aren't used to getting applications from nonprofits.

Panic sets in. The saddest part of it is that the panic could have been avoided.

The preceding passage contains five clues that indicate why Mr. Whetherbee is in trouble. He has violated basic rules of how to borrow. They're common mistakes, but the results can be lethal. His errors are:

1. Limiting to a bank his search for a lender
2. Doing business with a bank that is not accustomed to nonprofits
3. Failure to establish a close relationship with the potential lender before applying for the loan (the banker addressed him as Mr. Whetherbee, not by his first name)
4. Failure to allow the bank sufficient time to process the loan application
5. Providing incomplete information with the initial application

Even if you don't anticipate the need to borrow, you should develop a network that will be ready to lend. Your operations can change quickly, and the need may appear.

Success in borrowing may seem unpredictable. It isn't. Proceed according to the following rules and there's a strong probability you'll succeed if you need to borrow.

Know Your Financial Markets

Familiarize yourself with all sources for borrowing. Banks are only one type of institution that lend to nonprofits. In many parts of the country, foundations and government agencies lend to nonprofits. Insurance companies and other financial institutions also lend. Even private individuals lend. Each type of lender serves a different set of needs. Where you look for a loan should be determined by:

1. Why you need the loan
2. The length of the loan
3. The amount you need
4. Your ability to provide detailed information
5. The type of collateral you can offer (revenue contracts, real estate, reputation, etc.)
6. Your ability to absorb interest payments

Table 2.11, Lender Concentrations, shows the differences between lenders.

Look for Nonprofit Experience

Many lenders are afraid to do business with nonprofits; they don't understand fund accounting, feel that the management is amateurish, and fear they cannot foreclose a mortgage. It's unlikely that you will convince them otherwise. So find a lender that is accustomed to nonprofits. Government agencies and foundations with loan programs have considerable nonprofit experience. And many banks have special nonprofit sections. Try to find them before you need a loan.

Establish a Close Relationship with Potential Lenders

A major factor in the decision to loan is faith in the borrower's management abilities. Convince potential lenders of your capabilities before you need to borrow. One of the best ways to achieve this is to have potential lenders, or people close to them, on your Board. Board

Table 2.11
Lender Concentrations

LENDER	PURPOSE OF LOAN	LENGTH OF LOAN	SIZE OF LOAN	THOROUGH-NESS OF IN-VESTIGATION	EMPHASIS OF INVESTIGATION	INTEREST RATE
Foundations, Government	cash flow	short-term	small	medium	secure revenue	low
Banks	cash flow, capital	short to long-term	medium to large	very	colateral, long-term financial stability	medium
Other Financial Institutions	capital	long-term	large	very	long-term financial stability	medium
Individuals	capital	medium term	small to medium	very	collateral	high

members are constantly apprised of your financial situation. And they will have participated in the decision to borrow.

Another way to build a relationship is to meet regularly with potential lenders, such as your bank branch manager. Present and explain quarterly financial statements to them. Let them see how your organization is doing before you want to borrow.

From a lender's perspective the need to borrow represents either an inability to provide a product or service at its "fair price," creating an operating deficit, or it can come as a response to a reasonable growth opportunity. Show the lender, over time, that you have your current operations under control. You'll be more credible when you start talking about growth.

Allow Adequate Time for Applications

As soon as you detect a potential borrowing need, develop a timetable for applying. No one likes to borrow, so there is a tendency to delay until the final expected miracle doesn't happen. Often that's too late. Banks and other financial institutions often need up to six months to mortgage property. Individuals can take a couple of months. Government and foundation "bridge loans" can take six weeks.

A rushed borrowing application is viewed by the potential lender as a sign of poor management. It appears that you didn't know what was happening with your organization's finances. Start the process months before you need to borrow. Explain to potential lenders that you may apply for a loan and ask how much time they need to process the application. Develop your timetable in response to their answers—don't expect them to modify their timetables to meet your need.

Present Complete Applications

When you apply, ask the potential lender to specify the required documents. Supply everything that is requested. Failure to do this will slow the application process. It might even be reason for rejection of the application. Virtually any potential lender wants to see current, detailed financial statements as well as historical ones, going back over a few years. The format of the statements must be consistent to clearly show financial trends.

Even if it is not specifically requested, it is helpful to present a written application. Among the points that should be covered in this are:

1. A brief description of your organization's purpose, history, and current operations
2. An explanation of what you need the funds for and why you're borrowing to get them
3. Cash flow projections that show your ability to repay the loan
4. A list of your Board of Directors, including background information about them, such as their professions and employers

There are no guarantees that you'll be able to borrow when you need to. Capital markets are governed by supply and demand. At any time a lender has a certain amount of capital available to lend. It will go to the most desirable applicants. Depending on the amount of capital that the lender has available, it's possible that an institution that would be viewed as credit-worthy one day may be relatively less attractive the next. This is not because the institution has changed. Credit-worthiness is relative to the amount of capital available and the strength of other applicants.

You can't control the capital markets. But you can improve your chances of success in borrowing by researching potential lenders and presenting your request in a format they understand.

FINANCING CAPITAL ACQUISITIONS

6:00 A.M.—You arrive in the office to complete a major grant proposal. The Foundation must receive it by 9:00 tomorrow morning. You come in early to make sure that you finish it at a reasonable hour.

9:30 P.M.—After a day of nonstop interruptions, you're finally done with the proposal.

9:31 P.M.—Bleary-eyed, you crawl over to the photocopy machine to make the 84 copies that the Foundation requires.

9:32 P.M.—You press the button and pull the first copy out of the tray.

9:33 P.M.—Seven miles away they hear your screams. The copies look like tie-died T-shirts!

8:00 A.M.—At the copy center, you're begging the owner to make his machines perform miracles so that you can meet the 9:00 A.M. deadline.

10:00 A.M.—You're on the phone with the salesman who leased you the photocopy machine. He says that a repairman will come next month to fix it.

Doing your best to sound civilized you retort, "Why so long? I
can't live without it."

"You didn't take our standard maintenance agreement when you
leased the machine. So you're on a first come, first served basis after
the holders of service agreements."

You flash back to that fateful day you leased this wonder of modern
technology. You decided to forego the service contract. It cost $175
per month. It seemed like a lot of money.

"Then get me a replacement—a loaner."

"The only way I could do that is if you lease an additional machine."

"Okay, so pick this one up and bring me a new one."

"Sure. But, you know, that will be a pretty expensive deal. You
are obligated to continue payments on the machine you have for another 26 months. So, you'll be making double payments for the next
two years."

"But it's defective. I need a bigger machine. We're doing a lot
more copying now and this little machine can't handle it. When we
did this deal, you told me I could upgrade at any time—that I'd be
released from this lease without penalty. The difference in price was
about $30 per month."

"No problem, I'll have the new machine installed by noon. But the
increase will be more than $30 per month."

"What now?"

"When this lease was written, I told you this model would cost
$200 per month, or that you could have the super-duper X-10 for $230
per month. That was because we had a special sale on the X-10. The
regular price on the X-10 is $300 per month. I'm afraid that I have to
charge you that."

Sound familiar?

The same thing happens to hundreds of us every day with countless
products. You enter into a lease, thinking you've outsmarted the game
and won. Six months later, you find out who the real winner is. And
it's not you. But these problems can be avoided, by knowing what a

lease is (not what the salesperson lets you imagine it is) and evaluating its true merits.

Salespeople often use enticing financing arrangements to convince the consumer to take their product. So, many people confuse themselves by mixing their decisions concerning the merits of a product with the financing that's being offered. These are separate issues and should be analyzed independently.

A lease is one form of financing a capital good. It should be compared with the other forms of financing—cash payment and borrowing.

Virtually all major assets, from real estate to telephones, can be acquired through any of the three financing forms—lease, cash payment, or borrowing. In addition to considering the financing possibilities that the owner offers, take a look at options available through third parties.

Banks, finance companies, insurance companies, leasing companies, and private individuals will all consider applications to finance acquisitions. They can finance them through loans or leases. These sources offer better rates than the owner of the asset. They also allow the flexibility to finance a group of assets in one package, such as a single loan or lease to cover both a computer and phone system.

No finance package is perfect for every situation. Which will work best for you is determined by analyzing the advantages of each type of financing in relation to your needs at the particular time. Pay special attention to your cash situation.

The primary difference between the three financing options is ownership. With a cash payment, ownership is transferred immediately to the purchaser. No other party has an interest in the goods. When the money is borrowed, either of two things may occur, depending upon the terms of the loan. The ownership could be transferred immediately to the purchaser, in which case the loan would be unsecured. Or the ownership might remain with the lender, in the form of collateralizing the loan, until the debt has been paid.

In the case of a lease, the goods remain the property of the lessor. The lessee is paying rent for the use of the goods.

To determine which form of financing will work best for you, evaluate your proposed acquisition with the criteria in Table 2.12. Detailed explanation of the table follows.

Table 2.12
Comparison of Finance Forms

EVALUATION CRITERIA	FINANCE FORM		
	Cash	Borrow	Lease
1. Service	no effect	no effect	none to best (depending on lease)
2. Total cost of goods	lowest	moderate	moderate to highest (depending on lease)
3. Cash flow	worst	moderate	best
4. Credit line protection	best	worst	best to worst (depending on lease)
5. Activity restriction	none	worst	none
6. Inflation safeguard	best	best	worst
7. Obsolescence risk	none	none	worst
Balance Sheet:			
8. Current assets	worst	moderate	best
9. Longterm assets	best	moderate	best to worst (depending on lease)
10. Liabilities	best	moderate	best to worst (depending on lease)

COMPARISON OF FINANCE FORMS: EXPLANATORY NOTES

1. *Service.* The higher the probability that an asset will require maintenance and repair, the greater is the advantage to leasing. This is an important

factor with computers, photocopiers, and other technologically sophisticated machines.

   A. When the goods are financed with cash or with borrowed funds, the
owner assumes full responsibility for service.

   B. There are three leasing options.

      i.   Maintenance leases require the lessor (the owner of the asset—
the person or firm to whom money is being paid for use of the
asset) to maintain and repair the asset as well as to pay for
insurance and taxes on it.

      ii. Nonmaintenance leases require the lessee (the user of the as-
set—the person or firm who is paying money for use of the
asset) to maintain and repair the asset. The lessor pays taxes
and insurance.

      iii. Net leases transfer all ownership responsibilities to the lessee.
They may go as far as to require the lessee to assume responsibility for any loss incurred in the disposition of the property at
the end of the lease.

It is a common misconception, when leasing directly from a manufacturer, to assume that maintenance and service are included. This is
true only with a maintenance lease. However, with nonmaintenance or
net leases, it may be possible to purchase a separate service contract.

2. *Total cost of goods.* If your cash position allows it, you should acquire
assets with cash payments. It gives you the lowest total cost.

   A. A cash purchase is the least expensive, as there are no interest charges.

   B. If the funds are borrowed, the interest expense usually is less than if
you lease. Your down payment reduces the amount being financed
and interest rates are lower.

   C. There are two leasing options. They result in differing costs.

      i.   Operational lease. This is the most expensive lease, but it allows
the lessee the easiest escape. It can be cancelled at almost any
time, provided that the lessee gives proper notice to the lessor.
An example of this is a year-to-year real estate lease. But the
lessee runs the risk that the lease might not be renewed (despite
continued need for the asset) as well as a considerable increase
in the cost from lease period to period.

      ii. Financial lease. Any cancellation of the lease before its expira-
tion date must be approved by the lessor. These leases usually
have a longer term than operational leases, as the lessor often
charges the lessee the full value of the goods during the lease
period. As a result the monthly payments are usually less than
for operational leases.

For a nonprofit it can be considerably more expensive to lease assets than to purchase them, especially if the property is subject to taxes on an ongoing basis, such as real estate. Usually the owner must pay the taxes on the asset and the cost is passed on to the nonprofit. The nonprofit is unable to take advantage of its tax-exempt status.

3. *Cash flow.* A restricted cash flow can be helped by both leasing and borrowing.
   A. Cash payments reduce the buyer's cash reserves at the time of purchase. The full value of the asset is paid at the time of acquisition.
   B. Borrowing reduces the buyer's cash reserves at the time of purchase, but to a lesser extent than cash payment. A percentage of the full value of the asset (down payment) must be paid at the time of acquisition.
   C. Leasing doesn't require a large initial payment. The total cost is broken into installments, which are paid over the life of the lease.
4. *Credit line protection.* If you anticipate the need to borrow in the future and have established credit, cash payments and noncapitalized leases (see Section 4C, below) are the best options. If you need to establish credit, leasing can be an easy way to do it.
   A. Cash payments do not directly reduce available credit. But when you need to use credit, you have to demonstrate sufficient cash reserves to make the payments. So you have to be careful concerning how low you take your cash reserves.
   B. Financing reduces available credit. The amount you owe is an important factor in determining your credit-worthiness.
   C. Leasing may reduce available credit, depending on whether the lease is capitalized.

The Financial Accounting Standards Board (FASB) requires that a lease be capitalized and shown on financial statements if:

1. The lessee obtains title of the property at the end of the lease; or
2. The lessee may purchase the property at the end of the lease for a reduced price; or
3. The term of the lease is at least 75 percent of the asset's estimated useful life; or
4. The present value of the lease payments is 90 percent or more than the fair market value of the asset.

If the lease is capitalized it will show as an outstanding liability in the lessee's financial statements. This amount will be treated like any other outstanding debt and it will reduce the lessee's available credit.

5. *Activity restriction.* Restrictions placed by the lender on the borrower's future financial activities may make borrowing an unacceptable finance form. So you'll need to look at cash payment or leasing.
   A. A cash payment places no restrictions on future financial activities.
   B. Borrowing allows the lender to restrict the borrower's activities until the debt is fully paid. Examples of this are limiting the amount of additional borrowing, requiring a minimum bank balance, and providing a specified amount of insurance for the asset.
   C. Leasing places no restrictions on future financial activities.
6. *Inflation safeguard.* If you intend to use the asset over a long period of time, cash payment or borrowing is the preferable financing form.
   A. Neither cash payment nor borrowing increases exposure to inflation.
   B. At the renewal time of a lease the new price may be higher, due to inflation.
7. *Obsolescence risk.* An organization's needs may change over time, due to expansion or reduction of services. This may reduce the utility of an asset. And new versions of technologically sophisticated assets, such as computers, are continually being produced. The new models may be more appropriate for an organization. For these goods, leasing is the better option.
   A. Cash payment and borrowing do not decrease exposure to obsolescence risk.
   B. At the end of a lease term you can replace the asset with a more appropriate version.

Balance Sheet

8. *Current assets.* If the amount that shows in this section of your balance sheet is small, you may need to be showing more liquidity. You don't want to reduce the amount that shows in current assets. So you should definitely lease.
   A. Cash payment depletes current assets by the full acquisition cost of the goods.
   B. Borrowing depletes current assets by the amount of the down payment you make.
   C. Leasing has no effect on current assets.
9. *Long-term assets.* If you need to show more stability on your balance sheet, increase the amount that you're showing as long-term assets. Do this by financing with cash payment, borrowing, or a capital lease.
   A. Cash payment and borrowing transfer ownership to you, so the full purchase price is entered as a long-term asset.
   B. The effect of leasing varies, depending on whether the lease is capitalized (see Section 4C).

     i. Capitalized lease. The present value of the total of lease payments is entered as a long-term asset. An offsetting allowance is established for lease amortization. This allowance reduces the amount that is calculated in the long-term asset total, in the same way that depreciation does with an owned asset.

    ii. Noncapitalized lease. Not recorded as an asset.

10. *Liabilities.* If you have considerable debt, cash payment or a noncapitalized lease is the best option.

    A. No debt is incurred with a cash payment.

    B. Borrowing increases both current and noncurrent liabilities by the balance of the outstanding loan.

    C. The effect of leasing varies, depending on whether the lease is capitalized (see Section 4C).

       i. Capitalized lease. The total outstanding balance of lease payments is split between current and noncurrent liabilities.

      ii. Noncapitalized lease. Not recorded as a liability.

The form of financing used to acquire an asset will not affect the amount of satisfaction you receive from the asset. A photocopy machine will work or fail without regard for how you finance it. An attractive monthly payment scheme will not result in better copies. Two choices are required in acquiring the asset. The first is identifying which product will suit your needs best. Then, determine which of the available financing options is most appropriate for your organization. Follow this strategy and you'll get the most appropriate asset, obtained in the manner that is best for your organization's financial needs.

3   HOW TO SURVIVE YOUR AUDIT WITHOUT KILLING YOUR ACCOUNTANT

Few people can be as unsympathetic to the problems of small non-profit management as accountants. It seems they can't ever be satisfied that you're running your organization properly.

It's happened to many of us. You've finally provided the final schedule to your accountant to complete the audit. You breathe a sigh of relief, content that your problems are over. Unfortunately the real problems are just beginning. The accountant qualifies the congratulations for finishing with a hair-raising criticism:

It all adds up. The numbers are fine. But I'm very concerned about the lack of internal controls. I didn't see any evidence of wrongdoing, but you've got to be more careful. There are too many opportunities for theft. You've got to split up your financial operations—segregate the duties between different people.

"What a textbook answer," you think. How insensitive can the auditor be to the reality that your staff consists of one part-time book-keeper?

It's a real dilemma. You can't imagine how you can segregate duties any more unless you have additional staff. You can't increase staff unless you have more donations and grants. You'll have a hard time getting gifts and grants if a comment about the lack of the segregation of duties appears in the auditor's report. The fear of employee dishonesty can extinguish the donor's desire to give.

It's a problem. You need a clean audit. Donors and government agencies expect your financial statements to be audited. And, in many states, you must be audited to maintain your tax-exempt status. But it's becoming harder to get a clean bill of health from auditors. Fear of lawsuits is making them very cautious in their endorsements of small nonprofits. Increasingly, suits are being brought against auditing firms when a client organization discovers that it has problems. Recently a Big Eight firm was fighting a $100 million dollar claim that was brought against it by the Board of a California school. The accountants had failed to detect that the school's Business Manager had pocketed over $1 million in an eight-year period.

Accountants can limit the extent to which they certify the accuracy of the financial report. They do this by incorporating qualifying statements in the letter that begins the auditor's report. A "clean audit" doesn't contain any disclaimers. The opinion letter contains the following points:

1. The auditor has examined the balance sheet and related statements.
2. The examination included tests of accounting records, which were performed in accordance with generally accepted auditing procedures.
3. The financial statements "present fairly" the financial position of the organization and are in accordance with generally accepted auditing procedures.

The auditor's opinion may include disclaimers. These are what you're trying to avoid. Examples are:

1. *Scope Limitation*

The auditor wasn't satisfied that a certain part of the report was totally correct, but didn't believe that the problem was so serious that his/her opinion was invalid. In this case, the opinion letter states: "Except as explained below (an explanation of the problem will follow), our examination was made in accordance with generally accepted auditing standards." This disclaimer means that you couldn't provide adequate documentation to prove the accuracy of your records. Your internal controls are weak; they don't provide sufficient documentation to clearly establish that the revenue or expenses under question are accurately presented.

If the auditor believes that the internal control problem allows the possibility of significantly distorting the accuracy of the financial statements, the disclaimer is stronger. The opinion letter states that he or she is unable to express an opinion on the financial statements.

2. *Departure from Generally Accepted Accounting Principles*

The organization's records lack information essential to perform an audit in accordance with Generally Accepted Accounting Principles (GAAP). An example of this would be the failure to record the fair market value of a marketable security, such as a stock, on the day of receipt, despite the fact that there was information available for determining the value. GAAP requires that this information be recorded. In this case, the auditor's opinion will describe the break from GAAP with the notation that "except for the effects of . . . (the break from GAAP) . . . the financial statements present fairly the financial position of. . . ." This disclaimer is open to interpretation. It could represent a minor oversight that resulted from not being aware of the technicalities of GAAP. Or it could represent a significant lack of information. Fortunately, as the nature of the break is specified, it should be possible for the reader to interpret the disclaimer in its proper perspective.

3. *Inconsistent Application of Accounting Principles*

An important characteristic of financial reports is that they are prepared in a consistent manner every year. This allows clear tracking of financial trends. If the report format changes or if the technique used to compile the reports is altered, it becomes difficult to compare reports from one period to another and clearly identify trends. This can lead to the suspicion that the change occurred to hide something. In most cases this change would occur with your accountant's approval.

An acceptable example of a change would be to alter the value of a fixed asset, such as a building, to reflect a reappraisal of its value. GAAP requires that the value of fixed assets be shown at their acquisition cost. But this can significantly understate the wealth of an organization that has real estate that has increased in value over years.

The auditor must explain this change, so that readers will understand why the fund balance of the organization has changed. This is done by applying the changes retroactively with a prior period adjustment and noting these modifications. In this case the opinion letter will state that the accounting procedures are applied consistently after giving retroactive effect to the change in procedure.

Most accountants will discuss with you the reasons that they felt it necessary to limit the scope of their opinion. Unfortunately, few accountants will tell you how to fix the problem. They want to limit their exposure to a liability suit. If they don't suggest a solution, it's unlikely that they will be faulted for the solution that is implemented. It places a difficult burden on management to modify financial practices to meet the auditor's needs. But if you want to get a clean audit, you need to develop these techniques.

The two areas in which small nonprofits have the greatest problems are segregating fiduciary duties and documenting financial policies. This section gives you the tools to fill these gaps.

DEVELOPING REALISTIC INTERNAL CONTROLS

Segregating duties is the first step toward installing financial controls. It allows you to (1) demonstrate that the routine flow of financial activity in your organization contains sufficient checks and balances to catch errors and (2) reduce the possibility of employee dishonesty. How do you do it? If you have at least 25 different people in your accounting office, you won't have any problems. In any service organization there are 25 classic fiduciary functions. Ideally each task should be performed by a different person.

But if your staff is fewer than 25 people, you don't need to throw up your arms in despair. Even if your office only has two employees, duties can be segregated effectively. The crucial issue is hot you split the tasks, not how many people are involved in the financial processes. Who does what is the key issue.

Start by examining your operations. Complete the Fiduciary Function Worksheet as follows:

1. In the column of tasks on the left side of the page, write the names of the people who complete each task.

Table 3.1
Four-Person Segregation

BOOKKEEPER	CLERK	BUSINESS MANAGER	CEO
post A/R	mail checks	prepare invoices	sign checks
reconcile petty cash	open mail/ receive cash	give credits and discounts	sign employee contracts
write checks	record initial charges & pledges	complete deposit slips	perform interfund transfers
post GL	complete check log	approve payroll	approve employee time sheets
post C/D	disburse petty cash	approve invoices for payment	custody of securities
reconcile bank statements	authorize purchase orders		
	authorize check requests		
	distribute payroll		

2. In the row of tasks across the top of the page, write the names of the people who complete each task.

3. If any person appears in both a row and a column, draw lines through the chart from the row and the column to the box where they intersect.

4. If there is an X in that box, you have an unacceptable exposure.

For example, George prepares invoices (column 2) and disburses petty cash (row E). Locate the intersecting box. There is no X, so there is no exposure.

Polly reconciles petty cash (column 4). She also disburses petty cash (row E). There is an X where they intersect. This is an unacceptable exposure. Unacceptable exposures are danger signs. They indicate a process in which an individual's authority is unchecked.

It could be very difficult for Polly to detect mistakes she made in disbursing petty cash when she reconciles the petty cash report. No one's errors are harder to find than your own. Also, as Polly's dis-

Figure 3.1
Fiduciary Function Worksheet

	Complete deposit slips performed by	Prepare invoices performed by	Sign checks performed by	Reconcile petty cash performed by	Distribute payroll performed by
Post A/R performed by	✕	✕	✕		
Open mail/ receive cash performed by	✕				
Give credit & discounts performed by			✕		
Mail checks performed by			✕		
Disburse petty cash performed by			✕	✕	
Approve payroll performed by			✕		✕
Post G/L performed by	✕		✕		

Custody of securities performed by	Record initial charge/ performed by	Sign employee contracts performed by	Approve time sheets performed by	Complete check log performed by	Perform interfund transfers performed by
X	X			X	
	X				
X					
X		X	X		

Figure 3.1 (continued)

	Complete deposit slips performed by	Prepare invoices performed by	Sign checks performed by	Reconcile petty cash performed by	Distribute payroll performed by
Post C/D performed by	X		X		
Reconcile bank statements performed by	X		X		X
Authorize purchase orders performed by			X		
Authorize check requests performed by			X		
Write checks performed by			X		
Approve invoices performed by			X		

Custody of securities	Record initial charge/	Sign employee contracts	Approve time sheets	Complete check log	Perform interfund transfers
performed by	performed by	performed by	performed by	performed by	performed by

bursements go unchecked, she has ample opportunity to make false entries to cover any dishonest acts she may have performed.

Most likely you found your organization to be rampant with exposures. You scratch your head. It seems hopeless. The only answer is more staff. WRONG! While it is ideal to have each function performed by a different individual, clusters can be formed that reduce exposure. Tables 3.1, 3.2, and 3.3 provide some examples.

Before resting confident that the way you've assigned tasks will provide adequate controls, review the plan with your accountants. While they might not tell you how to solve it, they will tell you if you still have any unacceptable exposures.

Table 3.2
Three-Person Segregation

BOOKKEEPER	BUSINESS MANAGER	CEO
post A/R	prepare invoices	sign checks
reconcile petty cash	record initial charge/ pledge	sign employee contracts
authorizes check	open mail/receive securities	complete deposit requests slips
post GL	mail checks	custody of cash
reconcile bank statements	approve invoices for payment	perform interfund transfers
post C/D	distribute payroll	
gives credits and discounts	authorize purchase orders	
write checks		
approve employee time sheets		
approve payroll		
complete check log		
disburse petty cash		

Table 3.3
Two-Person Segregation

BUSINESS MANAGER	CEO
post A/R	sign checks
mail checks	sign employee contracts
write checks	custody of securities
post GL	complete deposit slips
reconcile bank statements	perform interfund transfers
post C/D	distribute payroll
give credits and discounts	reconcile petty cash
approve payroll	record initial charge/pledge
open mail/receive cash	approve employee time sheets
disburse petty cash	prepare invoices
authorize purchase orders	complete check log
authorize check requests	
authorize invoices for payment	

THE PAINLESS ACCOUNTING MANUAL

With the duties segregated, you're ready to develop an accounting manual. The manual provides procedures which:

1. Ensure proper documentation of transactions
2. Expand the segregation of duties to identify Board responsibilities
3. Establish timetables to prevent tasks from "falling between the cracks"
4. Set policies to reduce loss exposures.

"Why bother?" you think. Regardless of what your auditor says, you don't have any real problems with your accountability. An accounting manual is just icing on the cake. And it's going to take a long time to develop. It is true, creating an accounting manual from scratch is a major effort. But using the worksheets that follow, it won't take more than a few hours. And the savings that you'll realize will be well worth your effort.

You will:

1. Reduce the time that you spend with the auditor. Whether or not you have an accounting manual, the auditor needs the information. If it isn't written, you're going to have to explain your operations orally. That costs money—for both your time and the auditor's.

2. Decrease the possibility that your auditor will misunderstand your policies.

3. Cut the amount of time required to train new staff members. They'll have a reference manual that will reduce their need for oral instructions from you.

4. Diminish the anxiety (and the loss of efficiency that comes with it) of new staff members as they try to understand your operations.

5. Protect yourself—you'll have proof that you did your job. You had control procedures, should an irregularity occur.

The place to start is by identifying financial responsibilities restricted to your Board. You'll find many of these Board powers have been specified in your organization's constitution and by-laws. Others probably have developed over time and are recorded in the minutes of Board meetings. In addition, informal understandings might exist between the Board and staff that have never been written in any document. Discussing these issues with your Board increases everyone's awareness of the appropriate lines between Board and staff authority.

Complete the following worksheet (Table 3.4). For any "no" answer, note something special about your procedures that makes the control unnecessary. Your accountant may allow it as a mitigating factor. For example, you may have developed other controls that accomplish the same purpose, or it might not be applicable to your operations.

Develop your manual by turning the questions into statements. For example, with Question 6 ("Has the Board established a policy for the conversion of accounts receivable to notes receivable?")

—If your response is affirmative, you could state in the manual, "The Board shall establish a policy which specifies the conditions under which accounts receivable shall be converted to notes receivable."

Table 3.4
Board Responsibility Worksheet

		YES	NO	If "no," describe mitigating factors
1.	Does the Board approve the annual budget?			
2.	Does the Board have the authority to determine at which bank(s) the corporation maintains accounts and does it designate authorized signers on bank accounts?			
3.	Does the Board approve all contracts made for the corporation?			
4.	Does the Board approve all loans made for the corporation?			
5.	Has the Board established a policy which specifies to whom credit may be granted, for what purposes it may be granted, and a policy indicating procedures to be utilized for the collection of non-performing accounts?			
6.	Has the Board established a policy for the conversion of accounts receivable to notes receivable?			
7.	Has the Board selected the corporations' insurance broker?			
8.	Does the Board ensure that the corporation maintains adequate casualty and liability insurance?			
9.	Does the Board review the insurance coverages on an annual basis?			
10.	Are the corporation's financial reports audited on an annual basis by a certified public accountant selected by the Board?			
11.	Are there other areas of financial control for which your Board is responsible? If so, list them.			

Table 3.5
Staff Authorizations Worksheet

	POSITION TITLE
1. Who authorizes credit memos?	
2. Who issues cash receipts?	
3. Who opens the mail?	
4. Who prepares bank deposit slips?	
5. Who prepares invoices?	
6. Who prepares statements?	
7. Who approves requisitions?	
8. Who completes purchase orders?	
9. Who completes check requests?	
10. Who receives invoices from your vendors?	
11. Who authorizes cash disbursements?	
12. Who writes checks?	
13. Who signs checks?	
14. Who mails checks?	
15. Who disburses the petty cash fund?	
16. Who reconciles the petty cash fund?	
17. Who authorizes salaries and hourly pay rates?	
18. Who approves time sheets and employee terminations?	
19. Who approves the payroll preparation?	
20. Who distributes the payroll checks?	
21. Who posts the general ledger?	
22. Who posts the accounts receivable?	
23. Who performs interfund transfers?	
24. Who posts the cash disbursements?	

Table 3.5 (continued)

	POSITION TITLE
25. Who reconciles bank statements?	
26. Who records initial charges and pledges?	
27. Who completes the check log?	
28. Who signs employee contracts?	
29. Who has custody of securities?	

—If you don't have the opportunity to give credit, there is no need to mention it in your manual.

—If you have an equally efficient substitute control, explain it in the manual.

The next step is to identify which staff members perform fiduciary functions (Table 3.5). Most of this information can be copied from the Segregation of Duties Worksheet you completed earlier in this chapter. After each task write the position title of the person who performs it. If there are any tasks that are not part of your organization's operations, note "Not applicable" in the Position Title column.

Now turn the questions into statements. For example, your answer to question 29 ("Who has custody of securities?") could be expressed in the manual as "The Director shall have custody of securities."

If there are any tasks for which you noted "Not applicable," you do not need to mention them.

We're ready to move to the Journal Worksheet (Table 3.6). There are two levels of information required:

1. Do you maintain X journal?

2. If you do—who maintains it?
   If you don't—why not? (describe mitigating factors, as you did on the Board Responsibilities Worksheet)

Follow the same procedure that you did with the previous worksheets and turn the questions into statements.

Now we're ready to look at the forms that you use (Table 3.7). Complete this worksheet in the same manner as you did the Board Responsibilities Worksheet.

Table 3.6
Journal Worksheet

		YES	NO	If "yes," who performs task	If "no," describe mitigating factors
1.	Do you maintain a bill book?				
2.	Do you retain supporting documentation for all bill book entries?				
3.	Do you maintain a pledge log?				
4.	Are all pledges acknowledged in writing?				
5.	Do you maintain a petty cash log?				
6.	Do you maintain a check log?				
7.	Do you maintain an accounts receivable journal?				
8.	Do you maintain an accounts payable journal?				
9.	Do you maintain a cash receipts journal?				
10.	Do you maintain a cash disbursements journal?				
11.	Do you maintain a file of all original invoices and receipts?				
12.	Do you maintain a general ledger?				
13.	Do you maintain an inventory of all capital assets?				
14.	Do you maintain an inventory of the corporation's capital assets?				

Table 3.7
Forms Worksheet

	YES	NO	If "no" describe mitigating factors
1. Are your credit memos prenumbered?			
2. Are your checks prenumbered?			
3. Are your invoices prenumbered?			
4. Do you use a check protector?			
5. Do you use a one-write system for cash disbursements?			
6. Do you use a one-write system for accounts receivable?			
7. Do you use a one-write system for cash receipts?			

Turn the questions into statements to complete this section of the manual.

The next issue to address is the frequency with which you perform the control procedures. Complete the Schedule Worksheet (Table 3.8) to document these processes.

Follow the same procedure you used with the previous worksheets and turn the questions into statements.

The information provided in this step allows you to create a schedule to demonstrate compliance with the timetable. A form for recording this information is shown in Table 3.9. In the rows enter each of the tasks you scheduled on the preceding worksheet. Make copies of this form. Every time you perform one of the scheduled tasks, note it in the pertinent box. File the completed forms. They provide excellent documentation of your compliance with the schedule.

The next worksheet concerns your security procedures (Table 3.10). Complete it the same way that you did the others. Turn your answers to these questions into statements to provide this section of the Accounting Manual.

Table 3.8
Schedule Worksheet

	YES	NO	If "no" describe mitigating factors
ARE THE FOLLOWING PERFORMED ON A DAILY BASIS?			
1. Accounts receivable journal posted?			
2. Paid invoices cancelled?			
3. Accounts payable journal posted?			
4. Cash disbursements journal posted?			
5. Deposit your receipts in the bank?			
IS THE FOLLOWING PERFORMED ON A WEEKLY BASIS?			
1. Reconciliations of the petty cash fund?			
ARE THE FOLLOWING PERFORMED ON A MONTHLY BASIS?			
1. Statements sent to all accounts which show a credit or debit balance?			
2. Balance the primary journals?			
3. Unannounced checks of the petty cash box?			
4. Reconcile all bank accounts?			

Table 3.9
Control Schedule

TASK   DATE PERFORMED

	1	2	3	4	5	6	7	8	9	10	11	12	13	14	etc.

Table 3.10
Security Procedures Worksheet

		YES	NO	if "no" describe mitigating factors
1.	Do you prohibit holding funds to be deposited overnight?			
2.	Have you instructed, in writing, all banks at which the corporation has accounts, that all checks payable to the corporation may be negotiated only be depositing them in the corporation's account? If so, is a copy of these instructions maintained in the corporation's files?			
3.	Are authenticated deposit tickets retained in the corporation's files?			
4.	Do you prohibit signing of checks which lack complete information (date, payee, amount in numbers and words)?			
5.	Do you require two signatures on checks?			
6.	Are all cancelled as well as blank checks kept in a secured location?			
7.	Are the only checks made payable to "Cash" drawn to reimburse the petty cash account?			
8.	Are advance payments to employees prohibited?			

DO YOU, ON A MONTHLY BASIS:

		YES	NO	If "no" describe mitigating factors
9.	Examine paid checks to ensure that they are free of alteration for date, payee, check number, cancellation and endorsement?			
10.	Post the general ledger?			
11.	Provide reports to the Board which highlight variances in financial activity?			
12.	Reconcile payroll checks with other payroll records and examine endorsements on checks?			
13.	Review all insurance policies to ensure that they are current?			
14.	Compare authenticated deposit slips with the check and cash logs?			
15.	Compare customer account balances with their contracts?			
16.	Examine the balances on all statements?			
17.	Compare invoices with client contracts or other charge initiating documents?			
18.	Initiate collection action in accordance with your credit policy?			

Table 3.11
Personnel Policies Worksheet

	YES	NO	If "no," describe mitigating factors
1. Do responsible substitutes assume the duties of all employees who have fiduciary functions when the employee is absent? If so, are the substitute individuals whose performance of the functions does not compromise the segregation of duties?			
2. Must all employees who have fiduciary functions take annual vacations?			
3. Are known relatives employed only in positions which make collusion improbable?			
4. Are all employees who have fiduciary responsibilities bonded?			
5. Are all employment agreements, salary modifications, termination notifications and agreements and pay modifications written?			

The final worksheet deals with Personnel Policies (Table 3.11). Turn the answers to these questions into statements to enter them into your Accounting Manual.

At this point, you have a very thorough draft accounting manual. And it didn't take that long to write.

Caution: It's a good idea to have your accountant review the accounting manual before you implement it. Then have your Board approve it. You'll have their support when employees grumble about the additional paperwork and their perception that you don't trust them.

4 FORM FOLLOWS FUNCTION: BUDGETING

A budget can be a hindrance or a help.

It's a hindrance if all it does is tell you how much money has to come in and how much can go out. It restricts your activities. But a budget can be a great helper. It can be among the most powerful management and fund-raising tools available. It can provide criteria for program evaluation, demonstrate the efficiency of organizational structure, and provide concise justification for your fund-raising needs. The key to whether your budget helps or hinders is the format you use to present it. The data used to prepare it are the same regardless of format. How you present the data determines the usefulness of the budget.

There isn't a single format that meets all needs. Rather, there is a variety of formats that address specific needs.

A budget can be descriptive or analytic. Some formats merely describe where an organization's money comes from and the type of expenses incurred, such as personnel, office expenses, etc. They teach you almost nothing. At the other extreme, some formats, such as capital budgets, answer abstract questions concerning complex financial management issues. They provide calculations to analyze investment opportunities and guide financial decision makers in allocating an organization's resources. These budgets aren't for mass consumption, but they're among the most useful tools available to management.

The crucial issue in budget preparation is to address the concerns of the reader. Why is the person reading your budget? What questions should your budget answer? And what conclusions do you want the reader to reach about your organization?

In this section you will learn how to structure your budget to make it a management and fund-raising tool.

BUDGETS AND PROGRAM ANALYSIS

More and more everyone involved in nonprofits is demanding accountability. Donors, funding agencies, and the people using the services all need to be shown that you're delivering the programs they want. On top of this, accountants and the members of your Board's Finance Committee have their own concerns. Everyone wants accountability, but they all have their own definition of what it is.

Among the strongest proofs of your accountability is programmatic budgeting. It presents financial information in a format that answers the questions of the budget reviewers, regardless of their definition of accountability.

A programmatic budget is very specific. It shows:

1. Accountants that the way you've categorized expenses and revenue falls within the guidelines they use for financial accounting.
2. Donors and funding agencies that their gifts and grants will be used to improve programs that interest them.
3. Fee-payers that most (if not all) of their money is being applied to the service they use.
4. Finance Committee members that you're spending money in the most efficient manner.

The programmatic budget is multipurpose. It addresses the needs of different groups of readers and provides them with the information they need. It doesn't change the facts. It organizes data in a framework that allows the multipurpose analysis.

The initial work of developing categories for a programmatic budget and analyzing transactions to provide baseline data is substantial. But once you've done the setup, you can modify the chart of accounts to

Table 4.1
Sunny Day Care Center Enrollment by Facility

Center	Enrollment	Revenue
1	200	$600,000
2	350	$1,050,000
3	350	$1,050,000
Total	900	$2,700,000

automatically analyze transactions within the programmatic framework. It will not require any more work than any other budget preparation technique.

Start by categorizing your revenue as to why you receive it. Break it down into the smallest logical units. In the case of Sunny Day Care Center, this would be done as follows:

1. It charges $3000 per year for each child it serves. The total enrollment is 900, which is divided between the three centers as shown in Table 4.1.

2. It receives one grant of $300,000 per year, which is provided to fund a specific research project.

3. It receives $300,000 per year in gifts. These gifts are unrestricted. All written materials used for solicitation refer to both operating and capital needs.

These three sources of income are then combined into a single listing of revenue (Table 4.2). Now we do the same thing with operating expenses, starting with the line items from the chart of accounts (Table 4.3).

These categories came from a careful analysis of Sunny Day Care Center's spending. They reflect the different rents and staffing patterns that each center has, as well as the administration.

The allocation of some expenses may be a little difficult.

1. Administrative offices are located in Center 1, so they share a receptionist and cleaner with the center. A portion of the rent has been allocated to administration, as these offices would be necessary for the organization, even if none of the centers existed. However, the salaries of the cleaner and receptionist have not been split, as the time

Table 4.2
Sunny Day Care Center Revenue

FEES	
Center 1	$600,000
Center 2	$1,050,000
Center 3	$1,050,000
GIFTS	$300,000
GRANTS	$300,000
TOTAL	$3,300,000

they spend on administrative functions is inconsequential. It is conceivable the administration could function without these employees if it had to.

2. The Director of Admissions serves all three centers, so the salary is split between them.

3. Expenses that are not tied to a specific center, but are incurred on behalf of all centers, also are placed in the administrative category. While a change in the number of centers might reduce costs, the effect probably would be minimal. For example, the total insurance premium is $160,000. This is composed of $85,000 for the liability policy and $25,000 in property and casualty for each of the centers ($75,000 total). Appropriately, the expense is split between each of the centers and administration. The liability insurance premium would change very little if Sunny Day added or dropped a facility, as the insurance underwriter probably would claim that the risk is the same regardless of the number of centers. The possibility of loss of physical property (buildings, furnishings, equipment), though, is directly related to the amount of property owned.

The format is further simplified for external reviewers, such as donors and fee-payers, with whom you don't want to share all of the details. This abbreviated form, which appears in Table 4.4, makes the links between revenue and expenses more obvious. Reviewers who require more detailed information could receive this short-form budget with the long-form, detailed budget attached as an appendix.

The bonus you get with programmatic budgeting is that it helps to focus the attention of people both inside and outside of the organiza-

Table 4.3
Sunny Day Care Center Annual Expenses by Function

EXPENSE	ADMIN	CTR #1	CTR #2	CTR #3	RESEARCH*	TOTAL
Person-nel**	135,000	512,000	619,000	626,000	225,000	2,117,000
Director	40,000	0	0	0	0	40,000
Bus. Mgr	27,000	0	0	0	0	27,000
Psychol	0	30,000(1)***	30,000(1)	30,000(1)	210,000(7)	300,000
Dir. Dev.	25,000	0	0	0	0	25,000
Dir. Admis	0	7,000	7,000	7,000	0	21,000
Sec	15,000	15,000	15,000	15,000	15,000	75,000
Reception	0	12,000	12,000	12,000	0	36,000
Bookkeep	28,000	0	0	0	0	28,000
Teachers	0	320,000 (20)	320,000 (20)	320,000(20)	0	960,000
Assts	0	100,000 (10)	200,000 (20)	200,000 (20)	0	500,000
Cleaners	0	28,000 (4)	35,000(5)	42,000(6)	0	105,000
Rent	20,000	70,000	123,000	100,000	10,000	323,000
Utilities	5,000	10,000	25,000	30,000	3,000	73,000
Office Exp.	50,000	0	0	0	8,000	58,000
Ed. Sup	0	18,000	31,000	31,000	0	80,000
Insurance	85,000	20,000	20,000	20,000	0	145,000
Fund Raise	20,000	0	0	0	0	20,000
Food	0	34,000	63,000	63,000	0	160,000
House Sup	0	10,000	20,000	20,000	0	50,000
Misc	20,000	0	0	0	54,000	74,000
SUB-TOTAL	335,000	674,000	901,000	890,000	300,000	3,100,000

TRANSFER TO FUND BALANCE $200,000

TOTAL $3,300,000

*The research project has a separate office and personnel. The expenses shown in the budget are the actual costs for the project. They are not an apportionment of the organization's expenses.

**Usually, you show the specific breakdown of salaries (which can be related to specific positions) only to an internal audience (Finance Committee, accountant). For external reports (donors and fee payers) you show only the personnel line item.

***Numbers in parenthesis refer to distribution of employees in this category.

Table 4.4
Sunny Day Care Center Annual Operating Budget

REVENUE		EXPENSES	
FEES		PROGRAMS	
Center 1	$600,000	Center 1	$674,000
Center 2	$1,050,000	Center 2	$901,000
Center 3	$1,050,000	Center 3	$890,000
GIFTS	$300,000	ADMINISTRATION	$335,000
GRANTS	$300,000	RESEARCH	$300,000
		TRANSFER TO FUND BALANCE	$200,000
TOTAL	$3,300,000	TOTAL	$3,300,000

tion on programs that serve people. The budget connects the mission of the organization to its use of money. It helps people to think about money as a tool to provide services.

Programmatic budgeting helps reduce the tendency to view the budget figures as an entity unto themselves. The impact of spending on programs is clearly established. The ties between finances and services provided are inescapable, making it clear that budgetary modifications affect services.

Programmatic budgeting opens your operations to close scrutiny. It exposes you to many questions. People have the material they need to ask piercing questions. So, before you release the budget, anticipate their questions and be sure you have the right answers. If you aren't satisfied with your answers, the problem probably is in your operations, not your budget format.

You can prepare for this by drawing some arrows on the budget to fully understand how the sources and uses of funds are linked (Fig. 4.1). Some questions and possible answers that could come about from this budget are:

From the Donor

Q: Between the fund-raising line item and the Director of Development, you're spending $45,000, which is 14 percent of your revenue, on fund-raising— isn't this a lot?

Figure 4.1
Sunny Day Care Center—Uses of Funds

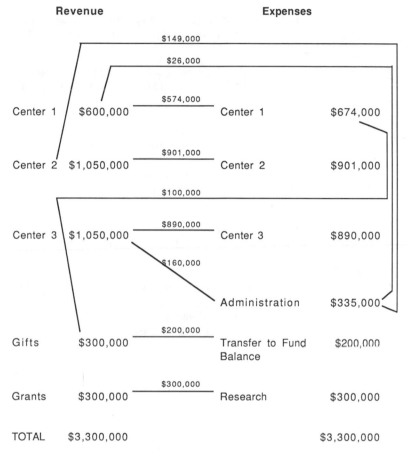

Revenue			Expenses	
		$149,000		
		$26,000		
		$574,000		
Center 1	$600,000		Center 1	$674,000
		$901,000		
Center 2	$1,050,000		Center 2	$901,000
		$100,000		
		$890,000		
Center 3	$1,050,000		Center 3	$890,000
		$160,000		
			Administration	$335,000
		$200,000		
Gifts	$300,000		Transfer to Fund Balance	$200,000
		$300,000		
Grants	$300,000		Research	$300,000
TOTAL	$3,300,000			$3,300,000

A: Fifteen percent is considered a normal level in nonprofits of our type and size. With that $45,000, we raise $300,000, which is a return of 7 to 1.

Q: Would you raise more money if you spent more on fund-raising?

A: This depends on your constituency; there's no standard answer to this question.

Q: What would the effect on programs be if donations fell 10 percent?

A: You can see that it would drastically effect the quality and scope of programs we offer.

Q: Where would you cut expenses?

A: Center no. 1, which serves a large number of disadvantaged children, is the most dependent on donations, so the cuts would have to be there.

Q: What is my donation paying for?

A: One-third of all gifts we receive go for scholarships for disadvantaged children. The remainder is retained to fund program expansion.

From the Fee Payers

Q: Twenty-five percent of my fees are being spent on things that don't directly help my child, like fund-raising to build capital. I don't think that's fair.

A: None of your fees are going for the fund-raising drive. It pays for itself. Your fees are used only to provide services.

Q: Your administrative expenses seem to be excessive. More of my money should be spent on my child.

A: Barely 10 percent of the budget goes for administrative expenses. In programs like this, 20 percent is considered normal.

From the Finance Committee

Q: Why the disparity in rents between the centers?

A: The facilities are located in different parts of town, where rents are different.

Q: What's included in miscellaneous?

A: Expenses that are small and do not fit into another budget category, like conference fees.

Q: Why are we paying so much for insurance?

A: We have been caught in the nationwide insurance crisis. We've shopped around and can't beat the premiums.

Preparing yourself to answer questions like this is a grueling task. But it makes the difference between an organization with credibility and one that doesn't have it. Often that credibility can be the difference between an organization that can attract funds and one that can't.

BUDGETS THAT INVITE DONATIONS

Your budget can persuade people to make gifts to your organization. It'll help your fund-raising efforts if it shows prospective donors that (1) your organization is stable, and (2) their contribution will increase your organization's capabilities to fulfill its mission.

Not every potential donor is interested in your budget. But major donors increasingly are concerned about how an organization uses its money. At the very least, your Board members arc interested and they and their friends are among your best prospects for major gifts.

Is there a universal form that works for fund-raising? No. Every organization has different strengths that will make it more attractive to potential donors. It's up to you to develop a structure that will emphasize your organization's strengths. The only thing that all budgets need to have in common is that they project total income and expenses. Beyond that, there's a lot of room for creativity. The challenge is to find a format that works for your organization. There are many factors to consider in how you present financial information, such as:

1. Whom you're preparing it for
2. What their interests are
3. Which of your activities you want to emphasize
4. Which of your activities you want to de-emphasize

Determine what you want the budget to say about your organization, then design it to communicate that message.

Rarely are the amounts an organization receives (its income) and the amount it spends (expenses) equal. In nonprofit accounting, the difference between income and expenses is called the ''change in fund balance''—the nonprofit's bottom line. The fund balance is the organization's accumulated capital, so a projected change in it shows whether the organization intends to add to its capital or reduce it.

The change in fund balance creates a zero-sum equation, which can be expressed as

$$
\begin{array}{ll}
+\$ \underline{\hspace{2cm}} & \text{Revenue} \\
-\$ \underline{\hspace{2cm}} & \text{Expenses} \\
+ \text{or} -\$ \underline{\hspace{2cm}} & \text{Fund Balance} \\
\hline
\quad\quad 0 &
\end{array}
$$

Two scenarios are possible in this format. The organization either makes or loses money. If it makes money, it is increasing its fund balance. This appears as:

$$
\begin{array}{ll}
\$900,000 & \text{Revenue} \\
-\$700,000 & \text{Expenses} \\
\$200,000 & \text{Increase in fund balance}
\end{array}
$$

This organization plans to receive $200,000 more than it spends. If this were the organization's first year of operation, it would end the year with a fund balance of $200,000. This is money that isn't needed for day-to-day operating expenses.

For an organization that is losing money, the fund balance change would appear as follows:

$700,000   Revenue
−$900,000   Expenses
$200,000   Decrease in fund balance

This organization will have to find an additional $200,000 from somewhere to make it through the year. It could use capital it accumulated previously or it could borrow from an outside source. Or contributions will have to compensate for this deficit.

Fund balance changes, whether they're increases or decreases, can be interpreted differently, depending upon the viewer's perspective. Here's how people in three different roles can interpret changes in fund balances.

The *manager* sees an increase in the fund balance as a sign of good management. It means that the organization is living within its means and has its expenses under control. To the manager, a decrease in the fund balance indicates poor management. The organization isn't controlling expenses. It's spending more than it brings in.

The *skeptic,* on the other hand, always looking for justification for criticism, doesn't respond positively to an increase in the fund balance. How can the organization be making a profit? It's supposed to be a nonprofit enterprise. If there's any money left over, it can't be fulfilling its mission. It's hoarding money instead of providing services.

There's no way to win with the skeptic, as there will be similar criticism of a decrease in the fund balance. The organization is chewing up its capital. It's acting irresponsibly and won't have the funds needed for a rainy day or for growth.

The *donor* might have either of two interpretations of an increase in the fund balance. It could be seen in a negative way, as a sign that the organization doesn't need money. It has plenty of money, so why make a gift? But the same increase in fund balance could be interpreted by the donor as a sign of stability. It is obvious that the organization is going to be around. The gift won't be going to a sinking ship.

Donors also could have different interpretations of a decrease in the fund balance. It could be seen as the SOS call that the ship is sinking. There is no sense in making a gift to a program that is going to vanish. Large donations often are spurred by the desire to buy a little bit of immortality. Money given to a disappearing organization won't provide that immortality. Or, the decrease in fund balance could be seen as a temporary problem that is going to turn around. In that case, the gift can make a real difference. It gives the donor the possibility to play God.

There is only one group of people, the donors, who might interpret the change in fund balance in different ways. So if the budget is intended to be a fund-raising tool, design it to convince the donor that this change in fund balance means that their contributions are needed and that you're not sinking. Do this by showing the donor that your organization is stable. Moderate the extent of changes in the fund balance. Radical swings are disquieting to potential donors.

Now we get to the creative part of budgeting. Using this approach, you design a budget format that emphasizes stability. Of course, your organization must be basically stable for its budget to portray stability. The way that you present data determines how obvious this stability is to the reader.

There are many techniques that can be used in creative budgeting. Here are a few examples of how the same activities can be shown in different ways to influence the reader.

Let's start with an organization that has a perfectly balanced budget—inflows equal outflows. This shows great stability, perhaps too much. Everything seems to be under control, so why should the organization be begging for donations? It would be more attractive to show the organization as a growing concern that is building toward the future. Alternatives that it could present might be those in Table 4.5.

The creative budget is not deceptive. Actually, it is more accurate than the traditional budget. Capital expenditures (major additions such as buildings, equipment, furnishings, and vehicles) represent additions to the fund balance and will appear as assets on the balance sheet.

Table 4.5
Growth Budget

Traditional Budget		Creative Budget	
$800,000	Revenue	$800,000	Revenue
-$800,000	Expenses	-$750,000	Operating expenses
0	Change in Fund Balance	+$50,000	Change in Fund Balance(to be invested in capital goods)

They will increase the fund balance and show the organization to be dynamic and preparing for the future. It's not just surviving—it's growing.

Another organization can't make ends meet. Expenses will be more than the earned revenue. How will it cover the shortfall? By fundraising. This can be shown in the budget (Table 4.6) and it will provide a much healthier picture. The strongest plea you can make when presenting the traditional budget is: "We have a $100,000 deficit this year. Help us to cover it." The creative budget is much more helpful in appealing to the potential donor. You can say: "This year's budget requires $110,000 in contributions. We need this to provide the programs and services we've planned." The potential donor should see

Table 4.6
Required Contributions Budget

Traditional Budget		Creative Budget	
$500,000	Revenue	$500,000	Service revenue
-$600,000	Expenses	+$110,000	Contribution revenue
		-$600,000	Expenses
-$100,000	Change in Fund Balance	+$10,000	Change in Fund Balance

Table 4.7
Future Investment Budget

Traditional Budget		Creative Budget	
$800,000	Revenue	$800,000	Service revenue
-$600,000	Expenses	-$600,000	Operating expenses
		$200,000	Excess over expenses
		+$100,000	Fund Balance at beginning of year
		Transfers	
		-$160,000	For equipment acquisitions (capital)
+$200,000	Change in Fund Balance	+$140,000	Fund Balance at end of year

the gift as a means to help provide excellence—not as funds required to cover managerial shortfalls.

An organization that anticipates having revenue far in excess of expenses will have a hard time fund-raising. Why should someone make a gift to it? It's doing all right on its own. The budget has to show how the extra revenue will be used for necessary projects.

The $200,000 increase in fund balance shown in the traditional budget is still there in the creative budget (Table 4.7). But now you can say, "We're investing in the future" (the $160,000 equipment will appear on the balance sheet as an asset). That's much better than saying, "We'll make 200 grand this year."

Now that you see the power of creative budgeting, a few words of caution. Don't set your projected contributions figure based solely on how much you need to balance the budget. The figure for contributions has to be realistic. Creative budgeting is a license to change form, not substance. If you set the contributions figure too high, you could end up with an embarrassing failure, a demoralized staff, and a budget that flops. If you set it too low, it could be very disheartening and lead people to question the usefulness of contributing. Project your contributions conservatively. How much can you realistically expect to raise? Then try to surpass what you've budgeted.

Before releasing any budget that doesn't show the bleakest possibilities, check with your accountant. Make sure that your efforts don't violate his or her bible—the GAAP (Generally Accepted Accounting Procedures). There are limits to creativity. Be certain that you don't violate them.

IS THE PRICE RIGHT?

Many nonprofit service organizations don't survive. After a few months, a few years, or many years, they die. They're out of money and are forced to shut their doors. "Too bad. They couldn't raise enough money. It's a shame they couldn't have found a better fund-raiser," say the sages. The blame is placed incorrectly. The problem wasn't the development officer. With few exceptions, fund-raisers aren't miracle workers. But they're expected to salvage situations that shouldn't exist.

The lethal illness, which causes the death of hundreds of nonprofits every year, is an inefficient pricing policy. Victims of this malady provide too much service for too little money. That's why their bank account shrivels and eventually dies. The organization's management designed the program they felt their clients deserved. The organization charged as much as management thought the clients could pay. Then they called on a fund-raiser to bring in the balance. The fund-raiser failed because the task was impossible.

Before making a panicked call to a fund-raiser, an organization should take a hard look at its pricing policy. Is it charging a fair price for each of its services? "Fair to whom?" you ask. What is a "fair price"? It's a price that is appropriate for both the organization and the client. It covers all of the costs for providing a service. If the entire cost of a service can't be met by the revenue generated at a given price level, the price is not fair. The organization has two choices—raise the price or discontinue the service.

This is a difficult decision. Nonprofits tend to view the value of a

Table 4.8
Happy Mental Health Clinic Programs and Services

PROGRAM	SERVICES
Training	application instruction
Group therapy	intake therapy sessions
Individual therapy	intake therapy sessions
Office rental	no actual services — just space

program in terms of the impact it makes on the lives of the people it serves. This is an important perspective, but its focus is very narrow. It ignores the economic viability of the service. Bills must be paid. To provide a program, you have to be able to pay for it with dollars, not with fund-raising projections. There's only one way to be certain that you can pay for everything you consume. It's by charging prices that are sufficient to cover the program's full cost.

Establishing a fair price requires a two-stage analysis. Start by identifying the services you offer. Break down the whole program into the smallest components possible. Then identify the resources required to provide each service and assign costs to them.

The Happy Mental Health Clinic trains therapists. As part of the training program, the students work with clients in individual and group therapy. Faculty members also rent offices from the clinic to conduct sessions with their private patients. The programs offered and the services required to provide them are listed in Table 4.8.

The next step is to identify all of the resources the clinic uses to provide its services. These data probably already exist in the form of the line items used in the organization's budget. Then the resources are classified as either overhead or service-related expenses.

Overhead costs are those that are not associated with the provision of a specific service. They tend to remain constant regardless of the volume of activity. Occupancy costs, such as rent, are an example. The rent on a building is set, regardless of how much the building is used.

Table 4.9
Happy Mental Health Clinic Overhead and Service Costs

OVERHEAD		SERVICE
rent	$18,000	electricity
Director's salary	$35,000	average unit cost
Adm. Asst. salary	$15,000	$0.15 per room per hr.
furnishings	$3,000	faculty salary. $50 per hr.
(depreciation)		clerical salary $10 per hr.
insurance	$8,000	cleaners salary $7 per hr.
office equip. rent	$4,000	
heat	$6,000	
TOTAL	$89,000	

Service-related costs change according to the amount of service being provided. Service-providing personnel is an example. There is a direct relationship between the number of clients and the number of service providers required. If a service were not offered, the center wouldn't incur these expenses. These costs grow in direct relationship to the quantity of services provided. The clinic's expenses are divided as shown in Table 4.9.

The resources included in the overhead cost benefit all of the programs. They all utilize these resources, so an equitable distribution of their costs can be established, spreading the expense between the programs. The one resource the Clinic provides to all of its programs is its building. The usage of this building becomes the logical basis for the distribution of the overhead expenses.

The overhead cost distribution can be calculated in two ways. One is to base it on actual usage—as the building is currently utilized, how much does each usage cost? The other is to base it on potential usage—if the building were fully utilized, how much would each usage cost?

In both cases we start by determining how much space is used to provide services. The cost unit is income-generating space—the space used for providing services directly to consumers, such as clients or students. We'll incorporate the cost for general use space, such as administrative offices, storage areas, and hallways, into this figure. Direct services, such as therapy and instruction, are offered in classrooms and therapy rooms. There are 20 individual therapy rooms, which average 200 square feet each. There are eight classrooms, which average 500 square feet each.

To allocate the overhead cost on an actual use basis, develop a schedule of room usage for a specified time period. Pick the smallest time period that includes the full cycle of any trends in usage patterns. For example, if a facility is utilized at the same rate every day, the time unit could be one day. If there are different use patterns over time, the specified time period must be long enough to include these cycles. For example, if a building is used less in the summer, the time period would be a year. In the Mental Health Clinic's case, the time unit is a year, as it operates at a low level in the summer. Its annual usage is shown in Table 4.10.

To establish the cost per square foot per hour, multiply the hours of usage by the space utilized and divide this figure into the total overhead cost:

$$\frac{\$89,000}{(200 \times 12,485) + (19,810 \times 500)} = \$0.0071 \text{ cost per square foot per hour}$$

Now we can calculate the cost per room per hour. Multiply this cost by the number of square feet in the two types of rooms.

200 square feet		500 square feet	
×0.0071		×0.0071	
$1.42	cost per hour for therapy room	$3.55	cost per hour for classroom

The potential usage calculation is considerably shorter. The total income-generating space of the center is:

8 classrooms @ 500 feet	4,000
10 therapy rooms @ 200 feet	2,000
	6,000 square feet

The clinic has an income-generating potential from 9:00 A.M. to 10:00 P.M. Monday through Friday. Discounting holiday closings, there are 200 days per year that the clinic is open, which means that there are 2,600 hours of potential usage per year (13 hours per day × 200 days = 2,600). The potential usage calculation is:

Table 4.10
Happy Mental Health Clinic Room Usage Schedule

Classroom	Hours used per year
1	1512
2	1423
3	1785
4	1832
5	1386
6	1280
7	1660
8	<u>1607</u>
	TOTAL 12,485

Therapy Rooms	
1	2012
2	1415
3	2386
4	2276
5	1852
6	1987
7	1831
8	1980
9	2043
1 0	<u>2028</u>
	TOTAL 19,810

$$\frac{\$89,000}{2,600 \text{ hours} \times 6,000 \text{ square feet}} = \$0.0057 \text{ per square foot per hour}$$

Once again, we calculate the cost per square foot per hour by the number of square feet in the two types of rooms to establish the cost per room per hour:

$0.0057	$0.0057
×200	×500
$1.14 cost per therapy room per hour	$2.85 cost per classroom per hour

Which calculation you use is a subjective issue. Clearly, you can't charge less than the potential usage cost. This is the absolute rock-bottom price. Your pricing level probably should be higher, as it is unlikely that you will achieve full usage on a sustained basis over time.

The actual usage calculation is more conservative. As long as you continue the same level of occupancy, you will break even. Extra efforts to increase space usage will be rewarded by surplus revenue. This calculation allows for the inefficiency of underutilizing the resource. It permits you to perform at less than 100 percent occupancy without losing money.

The cost per room is the base upon which we build the prices. To complete the calculation, we need to add the variable costs associated with each service. These variable costs, which are over and above the fixed overhead, are expenses incurred as a result of providing each service.

For the use of private office space, the costs are as follows:

Electricity: $0.15 per hour per room. This was calculated by turning on all lights in the building for one hour and checking the starting and ending meter readings. The number of kilowatt-hours used was multiplied by the cost per kilowatt-hour and divided by the number of income-producing rooms. It's not the most precise calculation, but it's relatively easy to perform and provides a reasonable cost figure.

Cleaners' salaries: $7.00 per hour. The janitors can clean three offices in an hour. Their average hourly salary, with benefits, is $7.00. The offices are cleaned daily, when used.

This cost structure does not lead directly to a precise calculation. The offices are cleaned once a day, even if they're used more than once in the day. The cost unit (day of usage) is different from the price unit (hour of usage). One way to resolve this is to establish a cost based on how much each office will be used. A fair guess would be 50 percent of the time. This would be 6½ hours per day. So the cleaning cost per hour of usage would be

$$\frac{\$7/3 \text{ offices}}{6.5 \text{ hours}} = \$0.35 \text{ per hour of usage}$$

Clerical salaries: $10 per hour. An estimate of the clerical time required by each office rental is the best we can do. For these purposes, it was established that the clerical time required to take phone messages, bill the therapists for office usage, collect their rent, and do the relevant bookkeeping, is one hour per month per therapist. The clerical employees' average salary, with benefits, is $10 per hour.

On the average, the therapists rent space ten hours per month. The cost of clerical service per hour of office rental becomes

$$\frac{\$10 \text{ monthly clerical cost per therapist}}{10 \text{ hours average monthly rental per therapist}} = \$1 \text{ per hour}$$

Add these amounts together to calculate the total hourly office rental costs.

$1.52	fixed cost
$0.15	electricity
$0.35	cleaners
+$1.00	clerical
$3.02	

The minimum charge for office rental should be $3.02 per hour. Market conditions probably allow a higher charge, so take advantage of it. Build a financial cushion. It will be there to help you if you rent the space less than you expected. If you exceed your predictions of how much you'll rent the rooms, you'll have surplus revenue to use for other activities. On the other hand, if market conditions don't support charging at least $3.02 per hour, the service should be discontinued.

The therapy program has two stages, intake and therapy. While they are related services, they can be segregated for pricing purposes.

The intake procedure for new clients requires two hours of clerical time for scheduling appointments, typing and filing reports, billing, receiving payment, and bookkeeping. The interview is conducted by a student, who is not paid. The decision concerning acceptance and placement of an application occurs in a 30-minute conference between the student and a faculty member, resulting in a cost of $25 ($50 per hour faculty salary × 0.5 hour). The intake process involves a one-hour interview with the applicant and the 30-minute conference. The space costs are the same per hour as for the office rental.

$0.15	electricity
$0.35	cleaners
+$1.42	fixed cost
$1.92	× 1.5 hours of office usage = $2.88 space cost per intake

The total cost per intake is:

$2.88	space
$20.00	clerical (2 hrs. @ $10 per hr.)
+$25.00	faculty salary (0.5 hr. @ $50 per hr.)
$47.88	

This cost schedule indicates that the clinic must charge at least $47.88 per therapy applicant.

Individual therapy plans average four one-hour sessions per month. The clerical time required for each client is one hour per month. The therapy is provided by a student at no cost, but the student has a one-hour conference with a faculty member after every four hours of therapy. The cost per session becomes

$$\frac{5 \text{ hours office usage} \times \$1.92 \text{ per hour}}{4 \text{ billing hours}} = \$2.40 \quad \text{space}$$

$$\frac{1 \text{ hour clerical} \times \$10.00 \text{ per hour}}{4 \text{ billing hours}} = \$2.50 \quad \text{clerical}$$

$$\frac{1 \text{ hour faculty} \times \$50.00 \text{ per hour}}{4 \text{ billing hours}} = \underline{\$12.50} \quad \text{faculty}$$

$$\$17.40 \quad \text{cost per hour of individual therapy}$$

Establishing the price for group therapy is more complex. The groups range in size from four to six clients, so a simple summation of costs won't suffice. The weekly sessions are 90 minutes long. They are given by a student, at no cost, who receives an hour of supervision from a faculty member for every two hours in session. The group sessions occur in classrooms.

The group therapy has flexible costs and revenue. Both will vary, depending on how many clients enroll in the group. We start by determining the minimum cost per group. This is separated from the increased expenses incurred by having more than minimal enrollment. The minimum cost per group is the fixed cost; it will occur regardless of the size of the group. The expenses that increase with enrollment are variable costs.

The fixed costs for the group therapy are classroom space, office usage (for the faculty–student meetings), and the faculty member's time. Regardless of the number of clients participating in a group, these expenses remain constant. The cost per hour of classroom use is:

$3.55	overhead
$0.15	electricity
+$0.70	cleaners (it takes twice as long to clean a classroom as an office)
$4.40	per hour

The fixed cost per session becomes:

$6.60	classroom space ($4.40 × 1.5 hours)
$0.82	office space (0.5 hour per session × $1.64 per hour)
+$25.00	faculty (0.5 hour per session × $50.00 per hour)
$32.42	fixed cost per session

The fixed cost per client per session is determined by dividing the total cost by the minimum enrollment of four:

$$\frac{\$32.42}{4} = \$8.11$$

The clerical time required per client per month is one hour, which equals $2.50 per session ($10 per hour/4 sessions = $2.50 per session).

This is a variable cost. It is a cost that increases in direct proportion to the number of clients served. If there are four clients in the group, the monthly clerical cost is $40.00. If there are six clients, the clerical cost rises to $60.00.

This expense is handled by establishing a break-even point—the minimal amount you can receive without losing money. It is the cost per client at the lowest level of enrollment. Using this figure ensures that you will be able to meet the fixed costs with minimal enrollment. The cost per client is established as:

$$\begin{array}{ll} \$8.11 & \text{fixed cost} \\ +\$2.50 & \text{variable cost} \\ \hline \$10.61 & \text{cost per client} \end{array}$$

The minimum price that the clinic can charge for group therapy is $10.61 per client per hour. If four clients enroll, the revenue generated will be:

$$\begin{array}{ll} \$10.61 & \text{cost per client} \\ \underline{\times 4} & \text{clients} \\ \\ \$42.44 & \\ \underline{\times 4} & \text{sessions} \\ \$169.76 & \text{revenue} \end{array}$$

The cost for the four sessions will be:

$$\begin{array}{ll} \$32.44 & \text{fixed cost per session} \\ \underline{\times 4} & \text{sessions} \\ \\ \$129.76 & \\ +\$40.00 & \text{variable costs (\$10.00 per hour} \times 4 \text{ clients)} \\ \$169.76 & \text{cost} \end{array}$$

At this minimal level of enrollment, the sessions break even—cash inflow approximates cash outflow.

If six people are enrolled, the revenues will be:

$$\begin{array}{ll} \$10.61 & \text{cost per client} \\ \underline{\times 6} & \text{clients} \end{array}$$

$63.66
 ×4   sessions
$254.64   revenue

The cost will be:

$32.44   fixed cost per session
  ×4   sessions

$129.76
+$60.00   variable costs ($10.00 per hour × 4 clients)
$189.76   cost

This results in surplus revenue of $65.00 ($255 revenue − $190 cost). The clinic can use this excess for other purposes. Regardless of the potential surplus, the clinic can rest assured that by establishing the minimal enrollment at four clients and charging at least $10.61 per client per session, it will cover its expenses.

The clinic's training program also has two components—application and instruction. They can be segregated for pricing purposes.

Individuals who wish to study in the clinic complete an application. The clerical time required to process each application is one hour. Three faculty members devote a 30-minute meeting to evaluating the application. Costs for each application are:

$10.00   clerical (1 hour × $10.00)
$75.00   faculty (3 faculty × $50 per hour × 0.5 hour)
          ───
                              2
+ $0.96   office usage ($1.92 per hour × 0.5 hour)
$85.96   2

Classes meet weekly for 12 weeks. Each session is three hours long. In addition to the class time, each faculty member is expected to spend two hours with each student in private meetings during the course of the term. The clerical work per class is estimated at 24 hours. Classes have a minimal enrollment of eight students. Fixed costs for the 36 hours of classes are:

$1,800.00	faculty salary (36 hours × $50 per hour)
$240.00	clerical (24 hours × $10 per hour)
+ $158.40	classroom (36 hours × $4.40 per hour)
$2,198.40	

The fixed cost per student becomes $2,198.40/8 = $274.80. Add to this the variable cost of $100 for the two hours of private sessions with the faculty member, and the tuition charge for each student should be at least $374.80 per term per class.

Applying this method of analysis to your organization, you can develop a price structure which ensures that each service you offer is paying for itself. Fund-raising activities can be restricted to developing new programs and providing financial assistance (scholarships) to individuals who can't afford the prices. Even if fund-raising efforts can't meet your expectations, your program should survive.

BUDGETING TO GROW ON

Expansion is exciting. New challenges await you. If you're successful—which you're sure you will be—you will take your organization one step closer to meeting its goals. It's satisfying.

Expansion also is very, very risky. The resources it requires can drain existent programs. It can drain them so badly that it destroys them.

Why take the chance? Why grow?

In nonprofits, we tend to answer this question with an idealistic statement about our organization's mission. There is an unmet need that must be filled. We exist to provide a certain service. The more service we provide, the more completely we are fulfilling our mission, our reason for being. Although this is true, it is not the complete answer. If it were, every social need imaginable could be met. If all that were necessary to solve a problem was to recognize it and design a program to solve it, society would be able to cure all of its ills. But it can't.

Society can't solve all of its problems because not all solutions make sense financially. To fully evaluate whether your organization should engage in a program, two criteria deserve examination. Determine if the program will (1) meet a social need and (2) increase your organization's fund balance. The second reason is as important as the first.

The financial impact that a program will have on the organization that sponsors it deserves as close scrutiny as the effect that the program will have on the lives of the individuals it serves.

It is not sufficient to show a balanced operating budget for the project. Minimally, the program has to be able to pay for itself. But it needs to do more. The program that you pursue should represent the best possible use of the funds that are available to your organization at the given time. The program has to be defensible in financial as well as service terms.

How do you know if a program makes financial sense? If it will improve your organization's financial position? By preparing a capital budget. This technique evaluates the financial impact of a project on an organization. It assesses the relationship between the cost of the project with the project's revenue-generating capacity. It compares programs to determine which is the best financial option available. The usefulness of capital budgeting is not limited to program expansion. It is a valuable tool to analyze any capital investment. You can use it to determine the financial benefits of expanding existent services, beginning new services, routine replacement of equipment and other assets, as well as replacement of equipment and other assets for cost reduction.

Start the capital budgeting process by preparing two sets of financial projections. How much is it going to cost to start the project—what is its initial cost? And you need to predict the cash inflows that the project will create. How much revenue will be generated and when will it be received?

Initial cost calculations contain all cash movements. Every expense associated with starting the project is included. For example, if you're acquiring a machine, all of the costs associated with the purchase are included—purchase price, freight, installation, and so on. If it is necessary to finance the acquisition, total finance charges are also added in.

The cost calculations are limited to cash movements. If you are replacing an old machine with a new one, a salesperson may offer you a reduced price if you trade in the old machine. Don't include this discount in the calculation—it is not a cash movement.

Here's an example of how initial cost is determined. The Useful Sheltered Workshop is considering replacing four knitting machines with new models. The direct cost for the four machines will be:

$27,000   purchase price
$2,200   shipping
+ $400   installation
$29,600

In addition to the direct cost for the machines, the workshop will require more working capital—the funds that must be available to maintain the new level of operations. The need for increased working capital could occur for a variety of reasons. It might be due to an increase
in billings, which would result in a higher level of accounts receivable
that the organization must "float." It could also come from an increase in supply inventory, or any other need that would modify the
amount of capital the organization needs to have available to meet its
day-to-day operating expenses. The increase in working capital is a
cost of the project. It is diverting funds from other uses, making it a
cost of doing the project.

   In the workshop's case, the only increased working capital requirements will come from additional supply inventory expenses. The old
knitting machines produced 16 square yards of fabric per hour. The
new machines will produce 24 square yards per hour. The workshop
currently maintains a thread inventory of $10,000. This will have to
increase by 50 percent to keep the machines going while maintaining
the same purchasing cycle. The increased working capital needs must
be met with cash, so they are added to the cost of the machines. An
expanded initial cost schedule is developed:

$27,000   purchasing price
$2,200   shipping
$400   installation
+$5,000   increase in inventory
$34,600   total cost of project

   The next step is predicting the net cash inflows the project will
produce. Calculate this by estimating the total projected revenue and
subtracting from it the cost of providing the goods or service. Annual
sales are projected to be 55,000 yards per year at $1.00 per yard,
resulting in inflows of $55,000. Labor and material costs required to
produce the $55,000 sales level are $40,000. The net cash flow is
$15,000 per year.

The one additional figure required to determine the value of a capital project is its projected useful life. Normally this is seen as five years for machinery and 20 years for buildings. Depending upon the nature of the specific asset, you might alter these lifespans.

With these projections, you have the data to answer the question, is the project worth it? Will it improve the workshop's financial condition?

A variety of techniques are employed to evaluate the relation between initial cost and cash inflows. Each focuses on different facets of the project. The more techniques you use, the broader will be your perspective concerning the effects of the project.

The simplest calculation is the payback period—how long will it take to recuperate the investment in the project? If the net cash flows are constant, as they are in the workshop's case, the payback period is calculated simply by dividing the initial cost by the average annual net cash flow. For the workshop, this is:

$$\frac{34,600}{15,000} = 2.3 \text{ years.}$$

This means that approximately two years and four months after the project begins, the investment will be recovered. After that time, the net cash flow of $15,000 per year becomes surplus revenue, which will increase the organization's fund balance. If the machines are useful for five years and the other projections are accurate, the project will generate $40,400 in surplus revenue in the first five years (total net cash flow of $75,000 − initial investment of $34,600 = $40,400).

If the net cash flows are not constant, the calculation is more complex. Start by plotting the annual net cash flows. The schedule in Table 4.11 shows how this could work for a project that has a five-year life and requires an initial investment of $20,000. The full $20,000 investment will be recuperated in the fourth year. The payback period is more accurately calculated by dividing the fourth year's net cash flow by the balance remaining after the third year (20,000 − 19,500 = 500). Divide this balance by the total net cash flow for the year in which the payback occurs:

$$\frac{500}{10,500} = .048$$

Table 4.11
Net Cash Flow Schedule

Year	Net cash flow (annual)	Cumulative net cash flow
1	4,500	4,500
2	6,500	11,000
3	8,500	19,500
4	10,500	30,000
5	12,000	42,000

Add this to the three years already passed and the payback period is 3.048 years, or about two weeks into the fourth year.

The payback period analysis only shows how long it will take to recuperate your investment. It does not indicate the overall effect that a project will have on your organization's financial condition. It doesn't allow you to compare the value of income stream that will be generated by a project with other investment opportunities. The total return on an investment is a crucial factor in evaluating the project's viability. Why is the total return so important? Because it shows whether the organization is making the best possible use of its funds. Is it using its capital to create more capital?

Two indexes are available to show return on investment: net present value (NPV) and internal rate of return (IRR). Each focuses on different aspects of the return on investment. NPV compares the income stream generated by a project with other opportunities for using the same capital. It does this by determining the average annual percentage return on the initial investment. This percentage is a common denominator that shows which option will better your financial status the most.

NPV is especially useful when two projects are competing for the same capital. It can be extended to compare the project's return with the interest that would be earned if the money stayed in an interest-bearing account, such as a money market. Another application of this analysis is determining the maximum interest rate that can be paid to borrow the initial cash investment and still show a positive return.

NPV is determined by using the present value of an investment. Calculating present value is a complicated mathematical process. But fear not—you don't have to do the math. It's been done for you and the results are presented in Table 4.13. You only need to do some simple arithmetic to calculate the NPV.

The underlying concept in NPV is the time value of money. A dollar received today is worth more than a dollar received in the future. The only accurate way to compare income streams is by taking into account when the funds are received. Two projects that have the same ratio of initial investment to total return may have very different percentage returns, depending on when the money comes in. NPV shows the effect of the timing of cash inflows by reducing (discounting) future cash flows to compare the return on the funds invested in the proposed project with the return that the same funds would earn if they were invested in another way.

Going back to the example of the workshop's new knitting machines, let's assume that the only advantage to the faster equipment is increased production. The only incentive to switch is that the change will improve the workshop's financial position because more fabric can be produced. There are no competing projects. So what's the purpose of calculating the NPV? The surplus revenue generated by the machine replacement would be used to provide additional scholarship funds to clients who are unable to pay the full cost of their rehabilitation program. The capital to fund the project will come from the workshop's endowment. The question is, will more scholarship funds be provided by the new machines or by leaving the funds in the endowment? The return on the endowment funds, which are invested in the stock market, is averaging 12 percent per annum.

To calculate the NPV, start by drawing a chart in which the rows are the years and the columns are the net cash flows, the present value factors, and the present value. The present value is the net cash flow multiplied by the appropriate present value factor. For the workshop, the completed chart is Table 4.12. The NPV is the total of the present values less the initial investment. For these purposes, the interest charge for borrowing the initial investment is not included—it would be redundant. In this case, the NPV is

$$
\begin{array}{r}
54,072 \\
-34,600 \\
\hline
19,472
\end{array}
$$

If the NPV is more than zero, the project yields a higher return than the discount rate that was used. The project should be accepted. It will

Table 4.12
Present Values of Net Cash Flows

Year	Net Cash Flow	PV Factor @ 12% (from PV table)	Present value
1	15000	.893	13395
2	15000	.797	11955
3	15000	.712	10680
4	15000	.636	9540
5	15000	.567	8505
		TOTAL	54075

produce more money for scholarships than if the capital were left in the endowment.

What is the actual percentage return on the project? To determine this, we use the Internal Rate of Return (IRR). It tells not only whether the project will earn more than a selected discount rate, but it also tells how much the approximate percentage rate of the return actually is. The problem with the IRR is that it is often difficult to calculate manually. The easiest solution is to use a computer program that calculates the IRR. Many hand-held calculators have an IRR function.

The one case where the manual calculation of the IRR is fairly simple is that in which projects have equal cash flows in every period. In these cases:

1. Divide the initial cost of the project by annual cash flow.
2. Look at the row in Table 4.14 that corresponds to the number of years over which you are calculating the return and find the number closest to the quotient of the preceding division.
3. Look at the heading for the column you are in. The percentage given is the IRR. In the case of the knitting machines, the IRR is:

$$\frac{30,600}{15,000} = 2.04$$

Looking at the five-year row in the table, the lowest factor is 2.99, which corresponds to a return of 20 percent. The IRR is in excess of 20 percent.

Table 4.13
Present Value

Period	1%	2%	3%	4%	5%	6%	7%	8%	10%	12%	15%	20%
1	.990	.980	.971	.962	.952	.943	.935	.926	.909	.893	.870	.833
2	.980	.961	.943	.925	.907	.890	.873	.857	.826	.797	.756	.694
3	.971	.942	.915	.889	.864	.840	.816	.794	.751	.712	.658	.579
4	.961	.924	.889	.855	.823	.792	.763	.735	.683	.636	.572	.482
5	.952	.906	.863	.822	.784	.747	.713	.681	.621	.567	.497	.402
6	.942	.888	.838	.790	.746	.705	.666	.630	.565	.507	.432	.335
7	.933	.871	.831	.760	.711	.665	.623	.584	.513	.452	.376	.279
8	.924	.854	.789	.731	.677	.627	.582	.540	.467	.404	.327	.233
9	.914	.837	.766	.703	.645	.592	.544	.500	.424	.361	.284	.194
10	.905	.820	.744	.676	.614	.558	.508	.463	.389	.322	.247	.162
11	.896	.804	.722	.650	.585	.527	.475	.429	.351	.288	.215	.135
12	.887	.789	.701	.625	.557	.497	.444	.397	.319	.257	.187	.112
13	.879	.773	.681	.601	.530	.469	.415	.368	.290	.223	.163	.094
14	.870	.758	.661	.578	.505	.442	.388	.341	.263	.205	.141	.078
15	.861	.743	.642	.555	.481	.417	.362	.315	.239	.183	.140	.065
16	.853	.728	.623	.534	.458	.394	.339	.292	.218	.163	.107	.054
17	.844	.714	.605	.513	.436	.371	.317	.270	.198	.146	.093	.045
18	.836	.700	.587	.494	.412	.350	.296	.250	.180	.130	.081	.038
19	.828	.686	.570	.475	.398	.331	.277	.232	.164	.116	.070	.031
20	.812	.673	.554	.456	.377	.312	.258	.215	.149	.104	.061	.026

Table 4.14

Present Value of an Annuity

Period	1%	2%	3%	4%	5%	6%	7%	8%	10%	12%	15%	20%
1	0.99	0.98	0.97	0.96	0.95	0.94	0.94	0.93	0.91	0.89	0.87	0.83
2	1.97	1.94	1.91	1.89	1.86	1.83	1.81	1.78	1.74	1.69	1.63	1.53
3	2.94	2.88	2.83	2.78	2.72	2.67	2.62	2.58	2.49	2.40	2.28	2.11
4	3.90	3.81	3.72	3.63	3.55	3.47	3.39	3.31	3.17	3.04	2.86	2.59
5	4.85	4.71	4.58	4.45	4.33	4.21	4.10	3.99	3.79	3.61	3.35	2.99
6	5.80	5.60	5.42	5.24	5.08	4.92	4.77	4.62	4.36	4.11	3.79	3.33
7	6.73	6.47	6.23	6.00	5.79	5.58	5.39	5.21	4.87	4.56	4.16	3.61
8	7.65	7.33	7.02	6.73	6.46	6.21	5.97	5.75	5.33	4.97	4.49	3.84
9	8.57	8.16	7.79	7.44	7.11	6.80	6.52	6.25	5.76	5.33	4.77	4.03
10	9.47	8.98	8.53	8.11	7.72	7.36	7.02	6.71	6.15	5.65	5.02	4.19
11	10.37	9.79	9.25	8.76	8.31	7.89	7.50	7.14	6.50	5.94	5.23	4.33
12	11.26	10.58	9.95	9.39	8.86	8.38	7.94	7.54	6.81	6.19	5.42	4.44
13	12.13	11.35	10.64	9.99	9.39	8.85	8.36	7.90	7.10	6.42	5.58	4.53
14	13.00	12.11	11.30	10.56	9.90	9.30	8.75	8.24	7.37	6.63	5.73	4.61
15	13.87	12.85	11.94	11.12	10.38	9.71	9.11	8.56	7.61	6.81	5.85	4.68
16	14.72	13.58	12.56	11.65	10.84	10.11	9.45	8.85	7.82	6.97	5.95	4.73
17	15.56	14.29	13.17	12.17	11.27	10.48	9.76	9.12	8.02	7.12	6.05	4.77
18	16.40	14.99	13.75	12.66	11.69	10.83	10.06	9.37	8.20	7.25	6.13	4.81
19	17.23	15.68	14.32	13.13	12.09	11.16	10.34	9.60	8.37	7.37	6.20	4.84
20	18.05	16.35	14.88	13.59	12.46	11.47	10.59	9.82	8.51	7.47	6.26	4.87

If the cash flows are not even, the only way to determine IRR manually is through trial and error. Use the NPV method described above. Try different PV factors until you find the discount rate that leads to the NPV closest to zero.

With these three simple techniques—payback period, NPV, and IRR—you transform your financial analysis from answering the question "Can we afford to do it?" to "Is this the best possible use of our money?" When you take the risk of investing, you'll know that the potential gains are the greatest possible. It makes the risk worth taking.

5 LOOKING INTO THE FUTURE: LONG-RANGE PLANNING

It isn't easy to develop a long-range plan. And it can't be done quickly. But it's worth the effort. A long-range plans adds years to your organization's lifespan by:

1. Preventing obsolescence. You anticipate changes within and outside your organization and prepare yourself to meet your community's new needs.
2. Strengthening your fund-raising base. People give more to an organization that has a clear vision of its future.

It also reduces your workload by:

1. Decreasing the number of difficult decisions you must make daily. You'll be a policy implementer, not a policy maker.
2. Avoiding crises. You'll see problems developing and be prepared to confront them before they become overwhelming.

"Okay, so a long-range plan is important," you say to yourself. "But where am I going to find the time for this? I already have more to do than I can handle. The last thing I need is more work."

A long-range plan is a lot of work, but not for you. It's a shared responsibility. Long-range goals are set by your Board, so staff members only guide the process and provide information. You guide the process by asking questions. Use the worksheets that follow. They'll help your Board to confront the issues that must be addressed to develop a realistic, useful long-range plan.

You probably already have most of the information you'll need. The missing data should be easy to obtain from government agencies, the chamber of commerce, and community development agencies.

Properly managed, creation of a long-range plan is not a great burden for staff. It's a group project that draws upon the resources of Board and staff.

Development of a long-range plan has three stages. They follow a sequence, as the plan is a cumulative building project. The stages are:

1. Defining why your organization has been successful
2. Deciding what your organization is going to be
3. Developing your strategy

WHY ARE YOU SUCCESSFUL?

Why does your organization exist?

The simplest answer is that it meets a social need.

Correct. But that answer is too general. There are thousands of social needs. Many are unanswered. Your organization deals with only one (or a few) of these problems. Why are you able to work with these problems and not others? Be more specific. Your answer to this question will provide a base for effective planning.

Another way to attack it could be by identifying who benefits from your program. Whose needs do you meet? Answer this question by turning it around: Who gives you the resources you need to provide services? Who meets your needs? Begin from the premise that there are no free lunches. Individuals and entities that give you something get something back for it. This exchange may not be obvious, but it does occur. You fulfill a need of theirs. In return, they fulfill a need of yours.

Who provides you with resources? Probably a combination of sources, which might include individuals who receive your services, other nonprofits (such as churches or foundations), individuals, and/or government agencies. Take the example of Gateway, a half-way house for the transition of retarded people from institutions to independent living. It receives funds from four different sources:

1. It has a contract with the state government.
2. It receives room and board payments from the residents of the house.
3. The resident's parents, in some cases, make the room and board payments for their child. Some are also a source of donations.
4. It receives grants from foundations.

Gateway exists to meet the needs of these individuals and organizations. Which of their needs is it satisfying?

1. For the state government, the program provides an opportunity for public officials to gain favorable exposure. The more publicity there is, the happier they'll be.

2. The residents of the house are able to gain dignity from their semi-independent living situation.

3. The residents' parents are able to alleviate guilt because they aren't caring for their child at home.

4. Foundations will be identified with a cause that will lead others to believe that the foundation is fulfilling its mission. As in the case of the state government, they will want to obtain maximum exposure from the project.

Gateway satisfies four needs for four different groups. Why does Gateway exist? For all of the above reasons. These can be synthesized into a ''needs-based'' definition. Gateway exists to assist retarded people to maintain their dignity and allow other individuals and organizations to demonstrate their support of dignity for retarded people. This needs-based definition sets parameters for a long-range plan. It allows the organization to continue serving the needs of its resource providers while adapting to changing conditions. It provides the latitude to expand current services, modify current services to respond to changes within itself and outside, and consider all services it could offer that might fulfill the needs of its funding sources.

With this example in mind, have your Board members complete the Needs Identification Worksheet (Table 5.1). Then, in a brainstorming session, combine their individual responses into a single list of re-

Table 5.1
Needs Identification Worksheet

Instructions: In the left hand column of the chart, identify our supporters. Who provides resources to us? These resources might be cash, technical assistance, gifts in kind -- anything we use to provide our services.

In the right hand column, describe what each of these supporters gets as a result of giving to us. Why do they provide us with resources? Stay away from "do-gooder" motivations, such as "they like us" or "they want to help the less privileged." Why do they like us? Why do they want to help the less privileged? What need of theirs are we fulfilling?

RESOURCE	RESOURCE PROVIDER (money, gifts in kind, etc.)	WHY DO THEY PROVIDE US WITH THIS RESOURCE?

source providers and their needs. Conclude the session by developing one sentence that synthesizes this information to explain why your organization exists.

WHAT DO YOU WANT TO BE?

The next stage in developing your long-range plan is easier. It's less interpretive; the answers are more obvious. You started by identifying the needs of your funders that you fulfill. To establish a goal, what you will be in the future, you first identify:

1. How you currently meet the resource-providers' needs

2. Why you're able to meet these needs

3. Changes within and outside your organization that will affect your future ability to meet these needs with the services you currently provide

The first point is very easy. How do you currently meet the funders' needs? By providing services. In the case of the half-way house, the service provided is the residential program. It's possible to imagine many other services that could fulfill the funders' needs of assisting retarded people to maintain their dignity and demonstrating to others their support of dignity for retarded people.

Why has this program been the answer? Because it's possible to achieve. The community in which it functions supports it. The community contains a variety of contributing factors that have allowed the program to come about. What are these contributing factors? They're any characteristic of the community which, if it changed, would affect the program. Examples of this are:

Demographics—How many potential clients are there in the area you serve? This is a very important component in determining the demand for your services.

Economics—How affluent are your funders and clients? Can they afford your services? Somebody has to be able and willing to pay for them.

Competition—Are there other organizations that provide an equivalent service in the same area? This might be another nonprofit organization, a profit-making business, or government-provided services.

Philosophy—Is the particular service model that you use in agreement with the ideological perspectives of your funders? What is the community reaction to your service?

Availability and affordability of resources—Can you get everything you need to provide your service in the area where you're working? Can you afford it? This refers both to physical resources, such as buildings, as well as human resources. Are properly trained staff available?

In the case of the halfway house, these factors contributed to its existence in the following ways:

Demographics

There are 47 retarded adolescents and adults in the catchment area who currently live with their parents.

Economics

1. The area's residents are primarily lower-middle-class, blue-collar workers who can afford this type of care.
2. The state has allocated budget funds for this program.
3. Six foundations have funds available to provide services for retarded persons in the community.
4. Clients receive disability payments.

Competition

There are no similar facilities that serve the area.

Philosophy

1. There is considerable support for community care of the retarded among professionals and government officials.
2. Lay community members tend to agree with the concept, but have resisted placement of the retarded in their immediate neighborhood.

Availability and affordability of resources

1. Staff is difficult to recruit at current salary level.
2. Adequate housing is available at affordable prices.

To identify the factors that contribute to your organization's success, ask your Board members to complete the Contributing Factor Worksheet (Table 5.2). Be prepared to research the current status of each factor, as Board members may intuitively identify and describe factors that deserve empirical verification. They may feel that something is important but may not have the objective information required to explain its effect on your organization. It's your job to describe the current status of the factors with facts and figures.

Now it's time to pull out the crystal ball. Go back over the list of contributing factors and describe trends you see. For example, are the demographics of the area, as they influence your program, changing?

Table 5.2
Contributing Factor Worksheet

CONTRIBUTING FACTOR	DESCRIPTION OF CURRENT STATUS
Demographic	
Economic	
Competition	
Philosophy	
Availability and Affordability of Resources	
Other:	

If so, how? In the case of the half-way house, they discovered the pattern in Table 5.3.

Ask your Board members to complete the Trends in Contributing Factors Worksheet (Table 5.4). Again, where necessary, you should do research to ensure that the Board's projections can be empirically defended. At this point, you have the data that you need to formulate your long-range goals. It's time for analysis. Concentrate on factors that appear likely to change. Analyze your ability to respond to the

Table 5.3

Gateway's Completed Trends in Contributing Factors Worksheet

CONTRIBUTING FACTOR	PREDICTED TREND	SUPPORTING EVIDENCE
Demographic	no anticipated change	number of retarded children and birth rates of retarded infants indicate that incidence of retardation in the area will remain constant
Economic 1. area residents	no anticipated change	the community is very firmly entrenched. It is too expensive for poorer people and not desirable for the more affluent
2. government support	no anticipated change	last funding bill passed 3:1 in the legislature
3. foundation support	decrease anticipated	emphasis of foundations changing to exclusively seed money
4. house residents	no anticipated change	disability payments are an institutionalized government program
Philosophy 1. Professional and governmental	no anticipated change	professional literature remains supportive
2. Lay community	increased support anticipated	as community gains experience with retarded their support of program increasing
Availability of resources 1. Staff	decreased support	job market expanding, forcing wages up
2. Housing	no anticipated change	no evidence of pressures to increase costs or decrease vacancy rate

changes. For example, if the level of a factor's support is increasing, look for growth possibilities. Does this change represent an opportunity for you to expand services? On the other hand, if the level of support is decreasing, how deeply will it affect your program? Can you compensate for the loss of support? How? Gateway has one increasing base of support—the acceptance of its philosophy in the lay community. Does this open any new program opportunities?

Returning to the needs-based definition of the organization, it exists

Table 5.4
Trends in Contributing Factors Worksheet

CONTRIBUTING FACTOR	PREDICTED TREND	SUPPORTING EVIDENCE

"to assist retarded people to maintain their dignity and to allow others to demonstrate their support of dignity for retarded people." Gateway could exploit this development to broaden its base of support. Efforts to do this would fall within the parameters established by the organization's definition of its purpose.

The decreasing supports are foundation funds and staff availability. Foundation funds represent 10 percent of the current operating budget. The Board felt confident that it could find the funds elsewhere, as the amount is so small. The availability of staff was felt to be a factor that could be improved by raising staff compensation levels. With this

Table 5.5
Trend Analysis Worksheet

Our organization exists to _____

_____

_____

Contributing factors which are predicted to change	Will the change increase support for our program?	If increase, how can we utilize the new resources?	If decrease, can we compensate? If no, should the program be reduced or terminated?

analysis performed, the organization's goals for the next five years could be stated as:

1. To continue to provide existent programs at their current level of services
2. To increase staff compensation to a level at which the wages and benefits are competitive

3. To develop additional funding sources for operational expenses

4. To encourage the expansion of the positive reception of retarded people in the community

The development of these goals is done by the Board. If you have provided the Board with sufficient data from your research, it should be able to design its goals without much additional input from you. Give the Board members the Trend Analysis Worksheet (Table 5.5) to help them structure the process.

DEVELOPING YOUR STRATEGY

This is the final stage in long-range planning. The dreams are converted into objectives and timetables are set for their completion. Staff does much of the work at this phase. It requires technical expertise. The Board's role is to suggest possible means for achieving the goals, and to review and approve the plans you recommend.

Have a brainstorming session to identify means for achieving the goals. Many ideas probably came out in the meetings at which the Board sets the goals. With the objectives established, additional ideas may come forth. To focus the process, have each Board member complete the Goal Implementation Worksheet (Table 5.6).

The next step is to set milestones—objective indicators of efforts to achieve the goals. How do you know that you're making progress? The goals you established are vague. Translate them into easily identifiable indicators, which will show that your efforts are directed toward accomplishing your goals.

Gateway decided to pursue its goal of encouraging "the expansion of the positive reception of retarded people in the community" by increasing their visibility locally and by developing opportunities for them to be seen as contributors to the community.

The Board decided that these goals could be met by securing employment for the house's residents in the immediate community. All residents who were competitively employed worked in the downtown area, five miles from the house. Most neighbors didn't realize the residents had jobs. They had no opportunity to encounter them in a work setting. The milestones that Gateway established for obtaining employment were:

Table 5.6
Goal Implementation Worksheet

Our organization exists to _____

_____

_____

We have chosen the following as goals:	How can we achieve these goals?

1. Development of materials that could be presented to potential employers showing the benefits of hiring retarded workers
2. Development of criteria for identifying potential employers
3. Identification of potential employers
4. Presentation of the proposal to hire retarded workers to potential employers

Table 5.7
Program Implementation Timetable

MILESTONE   RESOURCES REQUIRED

	Infrastructural	Physical Facility	Financial
Develop materials and criteria Start: 1/1 Complete:2/1	1/4 time position	none- can share office	salary of $5000 per year
Identify 15 potential employers Start: 2/1 Complete: 2/15	same	same	same
Present program to potential employers Start: 2/15 Complete: 3/15	same	same	same
Implement mechanism to identify job openings and monitor job performance Start: 3/15 Complete: on-going	1/8 time position	same	salary of $2500 per year

5. Implementation and maintenance of a system for obtaining information regarding job openings

6. Establishing contact between the house resident and the potential employer

7. If the resident is hired, monitoring the person's job performance weekly for the first month and monthly for the next 12 months

The implementation of the program requires resources. These can be categorized as infrastructural, physical (facilities), and financial (Table 5.7). The ability to provide these resources determines the feasibility of the goal. They must be available when needed. So deadlines are set for the occurrence of each of the milestones and they are analyzed with regard to the resources required to achieve them.

At this point you have everything needed to compile your long-range plan. Present it in the following format:

1. Organization's aims (you might include an abbreviated history of your organization in this section)
2. Identification of current support factors
3. Anticipated changes in support factors
4. Your responses to changes

It was lot of work. But now you and your Board have a common understanding of where your organization is and where it is going. It will make everyone's lives easier.

6 AVOIDING LAWSUITS WITH APPROPRIATE PERSONNEL POLICIES

What do you do when an employee isn't meeting your expectations? It's a painful discovery. Unfortunately, the solution may be even more painful. It can create new problems. Your organization is exposed to two serious threats—inefficiency and lawsuits.

One response is to work around the problem employee. Create a new position to fill the gaps. But paying two people to do the work of one certainly is not a very efficient use of funds. Another solution is for other employees to assume the weak member's responsibility. But this probably will cause them to burn out from overwork. You'll lose the productivity of good employees. Neither of these strategies is efficient. They circumvent the problem. You're paying for more service than you're receiving.

The only real solution is to confront the problem and terminate the employee. This rids you of the problem, but turnover is very expensive. Between recruitment and training expenses, replacing a professional staff member costs up to $20,000. For nonprofessionals the cost can be as much as $8,000. And this expense may be only the start of your problems.

The hiring and firing process is a Pandora's box. Once the box is open, you're vulnerable to employment discrimination suits. Perhaps you feel that you're protected from this since you don't discriminate. Unfortunately, that doesn't inoculate you from accusations of employment discrimination. Regardless of the validity of the charges, the cost of defending yourself against them can be astronomical. The financial threat is not limited to legal fees. The press might become interested in the case. A lawsuit can produce very damaging publicity. People don't want to be associated with discriminators, so the suit could discourage donors and funding agencies from continuing their support. It's not a pleasant scenario. You've rid yourself of the problem employee, but you could be facing massive legal bills and dwindling revenue.

There are no easy, inexpensive ways to solve these problems once they appear. But there are ways to prevent them or, at least, to minimize the risk that they will occur. This section provides techniques to use in the hiring and firing processes to reduce the possibility of hiring the wrong person as well as being sued for employment discrimination.

IS THIS REALLY THE PERSON YOU NEED?

You can't get everything you want in one employee. Each of us has a mix of capabilities we bring to a job. As obvious as this seems, many managers tend to make two mistakes when they're recruiting candidates for an open position: (1) wasting energy searching for the nonexistent candidate, the one who has all of the desirable skills and personality attributes, or (2) being lured by inviting attributes that aren't among those being sought in the first place. These problems can be avoided. Before you start actively recruiting, identify the most important skills and characteristics the person must have. This will be a shorter list than the one that enumerates everything you'd like this new employee to be. And you'll have some concrete criteria with which you can compare all of the candidates.

During the search you can change what you're looking for. If a candidate makes you aware of alternative solutions or opportunities you hadn't considered, you might consider them. But you'll be aware that they are alternatives—you're substituting a skill or trait you wanted with one you hadn't been seeking. You can weigh the advantage of the alternative against what you originally thought you needed.

Staying focused on your true needs is critical to making the right hiring decisions. It's especially important that nonprofits maintain this discipline throughout the search process for three reasons:

1. The cost of turnover is incredibly high. It makes sense economically to hire the right people. It could easily cost you $4,000 to hire a clerical worker, between running want ads, your time in interviewing, paperwork, and training. A professional person might cost $10,000. If you use employment agencies, the cost could double.

2. Most nonprofits are highly dependent on each of their employees. Typically, nonprofits are small, employing less than 25 people. The unanticipated loss of a staff member can throw everything else out of balance throughout the organization.

3. Nonprofits often are further distinguished by their inability to use compensation as a recruiting incentive. Most nonprofits pay poorly. Generally, people who work for nonprofits are motivated by factors other than salary. You have to find people who will continue to respond to the incentives you can offer.

Before you call the want ads or start passing the word that you have an opening, take a few minutes to analyze what it is you really need this imaginary new employee to do. Forget about all of the other things that you want the person to do. Unless you have very low standards, nobody can fit that bill, and you might be seduced by something that isn't really essential. In doing this, look at the person in their entirety, not just technical skills. The most articulate, intelligent receptionist is not so valuable if he/she regularly arrives at the office at 11 A.M. On the other hand, it might make sense to bend work hours for a great bookkeeper.

A good way to prioritize the skills and attributes required for a position is by completing the worksheet in Table 6.1. No more than three items should be noted as essential. With this general guide, you're ready to specify the requirements for the job. The skills and attributes you classified as "essential" are listed as requirements. The ones you noted as "somewhat important" become "helpful" criteria.

With the skills and attitudes prioritized, the next step is to identify specific indicators. For example, if you noted "educational level" as essential, what is the educational level required? Is it a bachelor's degree? A doctorate? Must the studies have been in a particular field(s)?

Table 6.1
Skills and Attributes Worksheet

	ESSENTIAL	SOMEWHAT Important	NOT VERY Important	IRRELEVANT
Physical appearance				
Style of dress				
Ability to do physical work				
Lack of disabilities*				
Clear speech				
Friendly				
Warm				
Firm				
Listening ability				
Ability to get along with associates				
Ability to get along with public				
Ability to work overtime or irregular hours				
Longevity of commitment				
Closeness of residence to office*				
Ability to work unsupervised				

Table 6.1 (continued)

	ESSENTIAL	SOMEWHAT Important	NOT VERY Important	IRRELEVANT
Initiative				
Work speed				
Work accuracy				
Educational level				
Specialized formal training				
Specialized informal training				
Lack of criminal record*				
Assume responsibility for others				
Ability to lead and teach others				

*These Items should not be part of your hiring decision unless they specifically relate to the individual's ability to perform the job. For example, you could ask and disqualify a convicted child molester from a position as a child care assistant, but you could not disqualify an embezzler from this position. The closeness of the applicant's residence to the office is relevant if the position requires that the individual be 'on call" for emergencies, which must be responded to quickly.

With these questions answered, the required educational level is expressed as "earned doctorate in clinical psychology."

Other skills and attributes can be more difficult to define. How do you know if someone can "assume responsibility for others"? One way would be to determine whether the person has supervisory experience. Are there other ways the person could show the same ability? What you accept as an indicator of this requirement is subjective, but you are noting that this is an essential attribute. The more specific and objective you can be with the requirements, the better. But it isn't always possible to find realistic indicators, so you may have to be more general.

The next step is to review the list of "somewhat important" skills and attributes and define their indicators.

List the requirements and helpful skills and attributes. Use this list to describe the job requirements whenever you publicize the vacancy. Later, when you're evaluating applicants, return to the list and record each person's ability to meet requirements as well as which helpful skills and attributes they possess. You have an objective basis for comparison that will keep your thoughts focused on the job requirements during recruiting and evaluation.

DEVELOPING HIRING PROCEDURES TO PROTECT AGAINST DISCRIMINATION

Hiring is scary. You're taking a chance. You're entrusting a virtually unknown person with part of your organization. Their failure will be your failure. The process of deciding whom to hire is even more threatening than most of us realize. It exposes your organization to the possibility of an employment discrimination suit. Most of us realize that hiring the wrong person could present serious problems. But rejecting an applicant for the wrong reason can lead to an even greater disaster. You could find yourself answering a lawsuit. This litigation might result in:

1. Mammoth legal fees
2. Valuable time in court
3. Bad press (which will quickly dry up funding sources)
4. Demoralization of your staff

An especially menacing feature of the U.S. civil justice system is that anyone can sue anyone for virtually anything. You can be sued, regardless of whether you've done anything wrong. And in employment discrimination cases, you're not always presumed to be innocent until proven guilty. According to the 1971 Supreme Court decision *Griggs v. Duke Power,* if employment practices seem to result in too few minority staff members, the employer is considered guilty of discrimination until proven innocent.

With whom do you have to be especially careful?

Virtually everyone.

Most people realize that racial and religious groups and women are considered to be minorities. They're legally protected against discrimination. But there are many more groups that require special handling. Technical, legal definitions of employment discrimination are abundant, but here's a simple explanation. You can be accused, with cause, of discrimination whenever you refuse employment to someone if the reason for rejection is not clearly related to the job requirements for the vacant position.

Your defense will fail if you claim that you refused employment to a member of a protected class (any group that has historically suffered discrimination, such as women, racial minorities, etc.) because your clients or other employees wouldn't feel comfortable working with the person. To be safe, your stated reason for rejecting an applicant must be based on the specific skills and attributes the job requires.

If the individual lacks skills or attributes that are essential to the job, you have a strong defense for rejecting them. Their minority status won't be the issue. For example, you're probably safe if you refuse to hire for a busboy position a person who is confined to a wheelchair. The person's handicap makes it impossible to perform the job. But the same person couldn't be disqualified from a position as a telephone operator on the basis of this handicap. Being confined to a wheelchair doesn't effect the person's ability to perform switchboard duties.

How can you protect yourself against employment discrimination suits? By focusing your evaluation of candidates upon the specific job requirements and ignoring factors that are not directly related to job performance. Begin this process by returning to the worksheet you completed earlier in this chapter. If you confine your interview to the items you identified on this worksheet, you'll probably do okay. While most discrimination laws are federal, state statutes may identify other protected classes. Again, the safest route, regardless of the jurisdiction in which the job site is located, is limiting your criteria to job requirements. Focus on that, not your fears of a discrimination suit.

Omit from the screening and interview process any factors that don't relate directly to the job requirements you established on the worksheet. Among the areas to avoid are the following, all of which have resulted in discrimination suits that were successful for the job applicant:

Age

Race

Sex

Religion (Religious groups and their subsidiaries, such as a church-supported school, are exempted from this. They may require membership in their religion as an employment qualification.)

Ethnic origin

Handicap (Any impairment that limits the activities of those afflicted with it. Chronic disabilities, such as paralysis or blindness, fit into this, but so do others such as AIDS and alcoholism, which are currently viewed as handicaps.)

Criminal record

Sexual preference

Two ways to protect yourself in an interview are:

1. Avoid direct questions that require the applicant to divulge membership in a protected class (any group that has historically suffered discrimination).

2. Ask all questions of all applicants. For example, if you are concerned that childcare responsibilities might cause a conflict between work and family duties, don't ask women if they have small children. Instead, ask all applicants about their ability to work overtime or irregular hours. That is the crucial issue. Your concern is scheduling flexibility. There could be many other reasons that an individual might have that restrict work hours.

There are many sticky situations, which could be viewed as discriminatory, but are not. The key to staying out of trouble, in addition to luck, is skillfully designing questions within the spirit of the law. Evaluate the applicant's abilities in relation to the specifically defined characteristics that the job requires. This is not condoning discriminatory practices. It's a technique to obtain essential job-related information in a manner that is less likely to be viewed as discriminatory. Here are some examples of how to do this:

1. A job exposes an individual to special opportunities to perform criminal acts of which they have been convicted. A convicted embez-

zler can be automatically disqualificd from a position that requires fiscal responsibility. In this case, the question that you can ask safely is whether the applicant has ever been convicted of embezzlement. You cannot ask if the individual has a criminal record. A drunken driving conviction is irrelevant to the job.

2. A job requires that an individual work on Sundays but the applicant's religious beliefs prohibit working on Sunday. If rescheduling the work would cause scvere hardship to the employer, the person's inability to work on Sundays may be a reason for disqualification. You have to separate the religious belief from the practice that interferes with fulfilling the job requirement. In this case, it is acceptable to ask if there is anything that would prevent the applicant from working on Sunday. It would not be acceptable to ask the applicants their religions.

3. Moving and lifting heavy boxes is an essential part of a job. You can ask the applicants if there is anything that would prevent them from moving and lifting heavy boxes. You cannot ask them if they are handicapped.

4. A position that involves considerable telephone work requires that the individual have a clear voice with good diction. This could be misconstrued by some people as a discriminatory criterion, aimed against members of minority groups who do not speak standardized American English clearly. But it isn't. You have a valid, job-related reason for requiring clear speech.

Avoiding discrimination suits isn't that difficult if you focus on job requirements. The most successful employment decisions are based on the specific skills and traits the job requires. Put on blinders. Stick to the job requirements. You'll reduce your exposure to a discrimination suit and you'll probably choose the best applicant.

GETTING MEANINGFUL REFERENCES

Reference checking is the most ignored part of the hiring process. Very few people take it seriously. Even human resource experts ignore it. Few textbooks on personnel management give the subject more than a page, if they discuss it at all.

In practice, many managers see reference checking as a waste of time. They've never learned anything from checking references. They don't learn anything because they don't know whom to ask for references, nor do they know what questions to ask. So the answers they end up with have the substance of cotton candy. All they get is "She was swell," instead of meaningful references.

There are techniques that transform the reference-checking process from a futile exercise into the most valuable facet of applicant evaluation. These strategies circumvent the primary obstructions to reference checking and provide meaty answers. Start the process by ignoring the traditional reference-checking procedure. Don't just call or write to a few people the applicant has suggested and ask the standard question, "What did you think of Mr. Hardworker?" There are two flaws in this process.

First, helpful responses usually come only from people you seek out. Rarely do they come from sources given by the applicant. And you can't be content with just recording the information that is freely volunteered by a reference giver. Many people avoid making candid statements. They're afraid that if they tell the whole truth, they could end up defending themselves against a lawsuit. Their fear is well founded. If the reference is negative, they could find themselves in court if your applicant feels that the reference is unjust. If they give an undeserved glowing or neutral recommendation, they could be subject to a suit brought by someone who hires the applicant and later claims that information was concealed concerning the individual's serious shortcomings.

So how do they protect themselves? By providing only name, rank, and serial number. But you can respond to their fears and help to overcome them. Then you'll get the information you need.

A helpful tool to quell the reference givers' fear of legal action for "unjust criticism" is a release form. They'll be more likely to talk freely if you have the candidate's written consent.

Include the form in Table 6.2 in your application. When you investigate a reference, you'll be able to assure the reference giver that the job seeker has consented to the interview. Offer to provide a copy of the signed release. With this signed form in hand, you're ready to go reference hunting.

The first rule in reference hunting is to treat the process as an extremely important part of the applicant's evaluation. Don't delegate this task to a secretary or anyone else. Do it yourself. When you're speaking with people who are providing references, make it obvious that you are interested in what they are saying. Respond to their com-

Table 6.2
Reference Consent Form

I do hereby authorize (your organization) to verify any representations made by me, either oral or written, concerning my application for the position of (job title). Further, I hold harmless any individual or firm for any information that it may provide. I understand that (your organization) may contact individuals or organizations other than those I have provided as references in this process. In addition, (your organization) has my consent to discuss with individuals or organizations other information which it feels may be pertinent to my application for this position.

Signature _____

Name _____

Date _____

ments. Ask for clarification of points that don't make sense. Request amplification of short answers. Make it obvious that you want their input—you're not asking them to just verify your impressions.

Be careful about whom you ask for references. Make sure that the references you get are coming from the right people. They are, in order of preference:

1. Your counterpart in the other organization. Hopefully, this person knew the applicant. The bond that you can establish with this person is important, even if this wasn't the applicant's immediate supervisor. Your peer is the most likely person to share candid impressions with you.

2. The candidate's immediate supervisor.

3. Your own contacts. If you find that people you know in the applicant's former (or current) organization or other organizations are familiar with him or her, these individuals will trust you. They'll be very likely to share frank impressions.

4. Additional resources that come through networking. Ask the people with whom you speak for additional sources of references.

5. Sources provided by the candidate.

The best ways to get references, in order, are:

1. A personal meeting. Take the time to meet with the reference givers. People are always more open in face-to-face conversations. You'll get nuances

that you couldn't obtain otherwise. The reference giver will be impressed with how seriously you're treating the process and will respond with the same seriousness.

2. A telephone interview.

The worst way to get references is through the mail. Aside from verifying name, rank, and serial number, these references are virtually meaningless. The respondent won't put much effort into completing the reference, as you haven't put much effort into getting the information. They will be guarded concerning the comments that they will commit to writing. And you won't have the chance to question their responses.

It's hard to start a free-flowing conversation in the interview. To begin the process, prepare an agenda you want to complete. Add questions and probe for deep answers as the opportunity appears. The form in Table 6.3 will be helpful.

One of the biggest differences that you will notice when you use this system of reference-checking is that you will obtain much more negative information than you got when you merely asked the question, "Was he or she a good worker?" The more you learn about the person, the more shortcomings will appear.

So how do you evaluate these newly discovered faults? By putting them in perspective. Think about the following:

1. An applicant should emphasize the positive when job seeking. They aren't being dishonest if they don't tell you everything. On the other hand, you should be very cautious of applicants who tell about their faults. If they talk so freely about their own problems, what will stop them from airing your organization's problems in public?

2. If you learn that a candidate was fired from a job, be aware that 80 percent of all Americans are fired from some job at some point in their lives. If you disqualify those who have been fired, you'll be fishing in a very small pond.

3. Competence is not necessarily shown through longevity in an organization nor advancement. That organization may value certain characteristics that aren't important to you. A great track record in one organization may merely indicate adept political skills.

4. Don't assign much weight to a singular negative reference. It

Table 6.3
Employment Reference Interview

CANDIDATE'S NAME _____

REFERENCE'S NAME _____

POSITION OF REFERENCE-GIVER _____

RELATION TO CANDIDATE _____

HOW WAS INTERVIEW CONDUCTED? _____

WHO SUGGESTED THIS PERSON AS A REFERENCE? _____

1. What were the candidate's dates of employment? _____

2. What position(s) did the candidate hold? For what time period?
What were the primary responsibilities?

Position title	Dates	Responsibilities

3. What was the candidate's initial salary? _____

Final salary? _____

4. Why did you let the candidate leave your organization?

(if "outgrew the position," then--"Didn't you have another job
for someone who is so good?")

5. What are you looking for in the candidate's replacement?

Did the candidate have these abilities?

Table 6.3 (continued)

> 6. I'm going to read you pertinent parts of the candidate's resume, which deal with his/her time in your organization. I'd appreciate your comments (record comments on photocopy of resume).
>
> 7. In what areas do you feel the candidate needs the most help with his or her professional development?
>
> 8. What type of people did he/she get on with best?
>
> Worst?
>
> 9. How would you rate the candidate in regard to the following --- excellent, good, average, sub-standard, or poor? (Review the list of the specific skills and attributes that you developed in the earlier section "Is This Really the Person You Need?")

could be vindictive. If one reference doesn't seem to fit in the trend, investigate further—establish its legitimacy.

It's a lot of work to get meaningful references. But the effort you invest in this process will be rewarded many times over. The probability of making a hiring mistake is greatly reduced. Spending a few hours getting meaty references is a minor effort compared with the time and money it takes to repair the damage done by a hiring mistake.

PREVENTING THE FIRING BOOMERANG

It's the ultimate good news–bad news story. The good news: after months of anguish, you finally fire the incompetent clerk. The whole office breathes easier. The bad news: a week later, you get a letter from the Equal Opportunity Commission. It demands your appearance at a hearing. You've been accused of employment discrimination by the clerk you fired.

It's the manager's nightmare. You've rid yourself of one problem, only to have it replaced by another. It's hard to tell which dilemma is more serious. The effects of a discrimination suit on a nonprofit can be especially disastrous. The last thing you want your potential donors to hear is that you've been accused of discrimination. They can become embarrassed by their association with you, so the discrimination charge can create an obstacle to your fund-raising that will have serious consequences.

You know you didn't discriminate. Your reasons for firing the clerk were justified. But now you have to devote your thinly stretched time and energy to defend yourself. What a waste of effort! The cruel fact is that employment discrimination suits can be brought against any employer who fires an employee. You don't have to discriminate to find yourself in a hearing room. Unfortunately, there is no way that you can eliminate this threat. It is the ex-employee's right to bring suit. But there are techniques you can use that will (1) reduce the possibility that a suit will be filed and (2) minimize the effort you need to defend yourself if a suit is brought.

All of these techniques must be utilized before you dismiss the employee. After you've fired the person, the only thing that can help is a good lawyer. There are three areas to analyze in relation to reducing your exposure to an employment discrimination suit. They are: reasons for firing, techniques of firing, and documentation.

Follow the guidelines presented. They can't eliminate the possibility of an employment discrimination suit, but they will reduce the probability that it will drain your energy.

Reasons for Firing

There are two acceptable reasons for firing someone. Either

1. The job they performed is terminated, or
2. Their employment was detrimental to the organization.

Getting fired is a great blow to one's ego. Some people will be vindictive, feeling that their dismissal was unjust. While your reason for firing someone may have been legitimate, there may be other circumstances that will provide them a basis for claiming that the termination was discriminatory.

An individual who is a member of a protected class (defined as any group that has historically suffered discrimination, such as women and racial minorities; while most discrimination laws are federal, state and local statutes may define other protected classes) might claim that minority status was the reason for the dismissal. People have successfully alleged that the following factors led to their terminations, making the firings discriminatory.

Age

Race

Sex

Ethnic origin

Criminal record

Religion

Handicap (any impairment that limits the activities of those afflicted with it; chronic disabilities, such as paralysis or blindness, fit into this, but so do others—such as AIDS or alcoholism—that are currently viewed as handicaps)

Sexual preference

A significant part of your staff probably are members of protected classes. If you fire them, they would be able to establish sufficient cause to sue you. It's a scary situation for an employer, but there are ways to reduce the effort required to stop the suit.

Techniques for Firing

How you fire a person can have a great effect on the probability that an action will be brought against you. The key factors in this process are

1. Moving slowly and cautiously
2. Giving the employee the benefit of the doubt

An individual who engaged in a grossly inappropriate act, such as embezzlement, must be fired as soon as possible. But there is little chance that this person would claim employment discrimination.

If the offenses are more subtle, such as failure to perform the job, you are wide open to a discrimination suit. Proceed slowly and cautiously. Be sure to give the person adequate opportunity to correct the inappropriate behavior. Try to let the employee feel that you have given him or her a fair chance. Proceed through the following steps:

1. When you discover that you may have to dismiss an employee, meet with the individual. Inform the person of your specific concerns ("You have been late for work seven times in the last three weeks"). Give the person a chance to explain why your expectations have not been met. It's possible that you could change something, such as working hours, to allow the individual's performance to improve. Without threatening, you should make it clear that failure to modify behavior could have serious consequences.

2. Close your meeting by establishing a time for a follow-up session. The second meeting should occur about two weeks after the first.

3. Between the meetings, pay careful attention to the individual's behavior, especially in the areas you discussed in the first session.

4. If the individual's behavior has improved to an acceptable level, offer compliments. There should be no need for a firing.

5. If the individual's behavior has not improved, the dismissal should occur at the second meeting. Review the specific areas that were discussed in the first meeting and make it clear that the termination is a result of the person's failure to improve in those areas. Confine the explanation to the specific job-related activities you discussed in the first meeting.

A very helpful technique to soften the blow of dismissal is severance pay. It can be considerably cheaper to spend a few thousand dollars at the time of dismissal than to pay the legal fees to defend yourself in a lawsuit.

Documentation

If suit is brought, you must be able to prove the reasons for dismissal. From the moment an employee's future is in question, document everything. For example:

1. After the first meeting, at which you present your dissatisfaction, send the employee a letter or a completed evaluation form, which indicates the specific problems. It should also note that a meeting was held to discuss the issues.

2. Make careful note of subsequent inappropriate behavior. You should describe the incident and note the date and time.

3. When you fire the employee, have a witness present.

Nothing can eliminate the threat of a discrimination suit. But these procedures improve the odds that it will be settled quickly. Also, it's a good idea to consult with your lawyer throughout the dismissal process.

7   POTENTIAL PANDORA'S BOXES

"Did you hear about . . . ?"

These words usually introduce a great joke, a rumor, or a business possibility.

Skeptical businesspeople realize that the money-making (or saving) opportunities that are introduced in this way often are indiscernible from jokes and rumors. How do they know which ones to follow up on? By carefully investigating the down side of the proposal before acting. Whoever is trying to convince you of the merits of change concentrates on the advantages. It's your job to imagine the down side—what could you lose if the supposed solution to your problem doesn't work?

Often we don't become aware of all of the risks until we've gone ahead with the project. Then it's too late. You've invested time and money in a venture and have to retreat. Aside from the monetary loss, the damage done by the failure to one's ego and professional reputation is painful.

Innovative, small nonprofits are especially susceptible to this problem. The promise of increased efficiency can entice the aggressive manager to take inappropriate risks. Take the example of computerization. It seems that every organization has a computer whiz who is

salivating at the possibility of automating the office. But many organizations don't have the tens of thousands of dollars required to buy
the appropriate hardware and software. So when the computer jock
says that accounting can be automated using the existent mini-mini
computer and buying only a $200 software package, the innovative
manager leaps at the opportunity.

What happens?

Sometimes it works, but not very often. More likely, the bookkeeper will devote tens or hundreds of hours inputting data and trying
to get the system to work. At some point, the manager realizes that
the printouts, which bear a startling resemblance to random number
tables in which the columns have been lost, are not meeting the organization's bookkeeping needs. The project is abandoned. The monetary loss has progressed logarithmically from the cost of the software
to include the fruitless pay to the bookkeeper. Hopefully, a manual set
of books was being maintained.

This section gives you guidelines for anticipating the down side of
three temptations that nonprofit managers commonly consider: payroll
services, buying consortiums, and nonrelated business income.

PAYROLL SERVICES

A simple way to reduce your administrative workload is to automate
your payroll preparation. You'll save a lot of the time you spend recording information and writing checks. You'll also reduce the possibility of problems with tax authorities.

There are significant differences between automated payroll systems. Carefully investigate the options available to you before making
the move.

Automating your payroll is a lot of work. But once it's done, it will
pay for itself many times over. The last thing you need to do is to
repeat the automation experience because you find out that your new
system isn't right.

There are two ways to automate: in-house and contracting a payroll
service. In-house services require that you have a computer. If you
aren't already computerized, it's unlikely that payroll automation will
provide sufficient justification to invest in hardware. However, if you're
considering computerizing your accounting, the possibility of automating your payroll should be an important factor in your decision.

Table 7.1
Comparison of Automated Payrolls

	IN-HOUSE	CONTRACTED SERVICE
Start-up costs	high	low
Start-up labor	high	low
Operating costs	low	high
Reliability	low	high
Security	low	high
Reports & W-2's	varies	varies
Tax service	no	yes
Ease of changes	varies	varies
Possibility of "final mistake"	low	high

Payroll services are provided by banks and specialized firms. They're the only choice if you aren't computerized and may be the better choice even if you are computerized.

Table 7.1 compares in-house automation with payroll services. Detailed explanations of the differences follow.

Start-up Costs

In-House—The payroll software can cost anywhere from under a hundred dollars to several hundred dollars. Usually the less expensive systems perform fewer functions than the more expensive ones and require more labor.

Contracted Services—Most are free of start-up costs.

Start-up Labor

In-House—There are costs associated with learning how to operate the software as well as inputting the data. If the software vendor or manufacturer offers considerable support services, the costs of learning to operate the software may be minimal.

Contracted Services—The only cost is the preparation of the data for initial input.

Operating Costs

In-House—Once functional, the only expenses for an in-house system are for materials and for the labor required to input changes.

Contracted Services—In addition to the cost of labor to input data, there is the charge for each run of the payroll.

Permanence

In-House—The loss of your payroll clerk can be a serious problem, as you may lose considerable efficiency while you train a new clerk.

Contracted Services—Your payroll service should have sufficient employees so that their personnel changes will not affect your efficiency.

Security

In-House—You need to develop and administer internal controls for the payroll system.

Contracted Services—While you have to check that transactions agree with the data you input, most payroll services have very strong internal controls.

Reports

The quality of reports produced by either system can vary considerably. Before deciding upon either system, request copies of all report formats and have your accountant review them.

Tax Service

In-House—The most information that any in-house system can provide is data for your reports.

Contracted Services—Many payroll systems offer complete tax service. They file your reports and defend them before the IRS if a problem occurs. This can be one of the strongest arguments in favor of using a contracted service.

Ease of Changes

The difficulty of correcting mistakes and updating files varies considerably. Talk with a few current users of a system about their experience in this area.

Possibility of Major Error

In-House—Should a problem occur with a payroll, you'll probably know about it in sufficient time to correct it before you must distribute the paychecks.

Contracted Services—A simple problem can have disastrous effects. If the payroll clerk doesn't catch it and incorrect paychecks are issued, you'll have little time to straighten it out before distributing the checks.

There is no perfect payroll system for all organizations. But for each organization there is a system that will offer more advantages than the other options. When you think you've identified the system that offers the most to your organization, look at the potential problems it presents. Weigh both the advantages and risks in making your decision.

BUYING CONSORTIUMS

Nobody likes to be laughed at. Especially when the person who is laughing should be trying to sell you something. It was so infuriating the time the voice on the other end of the phone said, "You think I'm going to give you a discount on how many light bulbs? Wait'll I tell them this!"

Or what about the arrogant HMO account executive. You were so certain that your employees were going to sanctify you for getting them such incredible medical care for so little money. Then that conceited drip politely informed you: "I wish we could help. Unfortunately, your organization is one-twentieth the size of our smallest client."

The one consolation is that you are not the only one who has had this problem. It faces all small businesses. In many places, the non-profit sector has responded by forming buying consortiums. They can offer three advantages: lower prices, reduced administrative costs, and access to vendors and services that otherwise would be unavailable.

Sounds great. In many cases, it is. But using a consortium results in losing some control of your procurement process. This might create more problems than it solves.

Why does this happen? Vendors give special attention to consortiums. Centralized ordering reduces the vendor's marketing and administrative costs. It will give the greatest incentives (price breaks, service, etc.) to the group that decreases these costs to the lowest point. The reduced marketing and administrative costs motivate the vendor.

Consortiums respond by centralizing the procurement process of their members to the greatest extent possible. The problem with this is that the more centralized the consortium, the less control is retained by the member of its own procurement process. The consortium can reduce the member's efficiency.

The savings that can be gained through consortium buying can be considerable. In addition to the lower price of goods, there may be great administrative and financing savings.

One of the "hidden costs" that could be saved through consortium buying might be the cost of labor required to locate products, order them, receive shipments, and to pay invoices. You won't need so much administration. This might make it possible to reassign your staff to reduce the number of administrative positions you need.

Another way in which consortium membership might affect your organization is by changing your working capital needs. The consortium might require that you pay bills quicker. You'll lose interest income and need to have cash available sooner. Or it could give you more time than your current vendors do. In that case, you'll gain interest income.

A third factor to consider in calculating your savings are the dues you must pay the consortium. After you pay the dues, are the discounts worth it?

Taking the above into account, you may determine that consortium membership is right for you. But don't send the membership application yet. There are nonfinancial factors to consider. Group buying can bring considerable savings in cash and administrative labor. But it also can create problems, such as:

1. Unavailability of the products you want
2. Delayed receipt of goods. This is a problem, especially when orders must be placed through the consortium's office and/or the goods are distributed through the consortium's office.
3. Unreliable product availability due to changes in vendors

Take time to carefully consider joining a consortium. A hasty decision may be very painful to correct. Group buying should allow you to save money on the cost of goods and services and it should streamline your administrative operations by shifting some of your workload to the consortium. But if you later drop out of the group, it could be very expensive to rebuild your administrative structure.

Most consortium drop-outs leave because they have to forfeit too much control of their procurement process. So before you join a buying group, investigate how much control you will be sacrificing. Call some current members and ask them the questions that appear in the Consortium Questionnaire (Table 7.2). After speaking with the consortium members, you will have a clearer idea of how much autonomy you'll have to sacrifice. The decision to join becomes more complex than a simple no-strings-attached offer to save money. The issue you have to resolve is whether the savings are worth it to your organization.

NONRELATED BUSINESS INCOME

Every day, more nonprofits are seizing the opportunities offered by nonrelated business income ventures—money generated by activities other than those for which the organization was established. These activities are as varied as the NPOs that sponsor them, but some of the better-known examples are gift shops and dealing in real estate.

But are these enterprises really such great supplements to traditional sources of income (fees, donations, grants)? When they're successful, nonrelated business (NRB) ventures create a powerful funding source. The income received from museum shops, university bookstores, and similar ventures makes dramatic differences for the nonprofits involved. It provides them with resources to offer services they couldn't otherwise.

Sounds great. Why not do it? Because you might fail. You might fail so completely that you'll threaten or destroy your organization's ability to provide the services for which it was established. There are two primary reasons that NRB income ventures fail:

1. The enterprise doesn't make money—it's a business failure.
2. Ignorance of tax laws results in unanticipated expenses or loss of the organization's nonprofit status.

Table 7.2
Consortium Questionnaire

	YES	NO	COMMENTS
Product Selection			
1. Do you have direct contact with vendors?			
2. Have you been able to get all of your normal brands of merchandise through the consortium? if no -- were the replacement brands of equal or superior quality?			
3. Have you been able to use vendors who you couldn't have used without consortium membership?			
4. Does the consortium search for vendors of a particular product or service you need?			
Ordering			
5. Do you place your orders directly with vendors?			
Delivery			
6. Have vendors provided goods and services you've ordered as quickly and as accurately as non-consortium vendors did?			
7. Are orders delivered directly from the vendors to you?			
8. Are the same vendors available to you on a consistent basis through the consortium?			
Service			
9. Do you arrange the servicing of products directly with the provider of the service? Or do you need to go through the consortium invoicing?			

Table 7.2 (continued)

	YES	NO	COMMENTS
10. Do you receive invoices directly from the vendor? if no --			
a. is the vendor's invoice made out directly to the consortium?			
b. do you have less time between placing an order and the due date of the invoice than you did with non-consortium vendors?			
c. if the invoice you receive is from the consortium, is the detail provided sufficient to establish an audit trail easily?			

Before launching an NRB venture, be realistic about your chances for success. You're going into new territory, which has its own rules. Be sure you'll succeed playing by these different rules.

The first area to examine is the probability of business success. In the conventional business world, two-thirds of new ventures fold in the first year. Why should you expect better results? To evaluate the business risks involved, ask the following questions.

What Advantage Do You Have Over Your Competitors?

Is the product or service you're offering either

a. unavailable in the target market, or
b. priced lower than that of your competitors, or
c. of higher quality than that your competitors offer

If you can't do one of the above, don't enter into the venture. Your product has to sell on its own merits. Don't kid yourself by thinking that people will buy from you because they like you. Your venture must fill a need of the consumer, not just your need for money.

One often overstated advantage that all nonprofits share is their favorable tax status. Usually it doesn't count for much in nonrelated business ventures, except if you're able to avoid real estate taxes on income-generating property. The tax advantages you might have shouldn't be the only justification for entering the project. You're looking for revenue, not a tax shelter. In addition, the IRS is responding to the claims of unfair competition from commercial ventures and becoming less accommodating to nonprofits in these areas. So you could enter into what is a sound business venture today, only to have the tax advantages taken away in the future. Would you be able to sustain the loss?

Is the Market Big Enough for Your Product?

Get expert advice on this one. You have a hunch that something will sell. Your friends and colleagues might say that they'll buy it. Is that a sufficient market? Spend a few thousand dollars on the services of a market research firm. It might prevent a much bigger loss.

Do You Have Sufficient Capital?

The primary cause of new business failures is undercapitalization. Make sure that you have access to sufficient capital to cover a slower payback period than your worst-case projection. This is a great opportunity for fund-raising—many business-minded donors will be more likely to give seed money for a project that will generate income than they are to give to cover operating losses.

Do You Have Access to Sufficient People Power to Carry It Out?

To protect yourself, be conservative and pessimistic in projecting your ability to provide the required human resources. Use the same caution as you did in predicting capital needs.

Does This Project Offer the Highest Return Possible on Your Capital?

Is the potential return from this project worth the risk? Calculate the rate of return, using the techniques presented in Chapter 4. Compare this return with other options available to you. Could you invest in the stock market and earn a similar return with more security?

If you're convinced that the project will succeed, look at the tax implications before proceeding. Aside from business failure, this is the primary cause of NRB flops. The best-designed plans for NRB income can be killed by the IRS. Structure your venture to minimize later problems with the government.

Two considerations need to enter your planning. You might be subject to NRB income tax, a cost that can raise your expenses considerably. The other possibility is that you could lose your tax exemption. Your organization received a tax exemption to provide a certain service. But this doesn't mean that any activity in which you engage will be nontaxable. The only universal rule of tax liability is that the income of for-profit enterprises is always taxed. The income of nonprofits is sometimes taxed.

How do you know if your enterprise will be taxable? The most certain way to answer this is with expert advice. Get an opinion from a lawyer or accountant, who has experience in this area of IRS case rulings. The criteria they'll be using is the IRS definition of NRB income.

The IRS uses three tests to determine if receipts are subject to NRB income tax. The income must:

1. Be received from a trade or business activity,

which is

2. Regularly conducted

and

3. Is not related to the exempt purpose of the organization.

The first test, that the income must be received from a trade or business activity, doesn't have many loopholes. The IRS tends to view "trade or business activity" as synonymous with "income-generating activity." Anything that produces revenue can fall into this definition.

There's more hope for escaping taxation with the "regularly conducted" test. The trade or business in which you engage must be an ongoing activity. This excludes many typical nonprofit fund-raising events. For example, selling ads in a program for an annual charity ball is probably exempt from this requirement. It is an irregular activity—the organization doesn't do it on an ongoing basis.

THE NONPROFIT PROBLEM SOLVER

The "regularly conducted" test could be a problem for an organization that has weekly bake sales. One way it probably could work around this would be to alternate the bake sales with other fund-raising activities. It could have a bake sale one week, a car wash the next, a dinner the third week, and then have another bake sale.

The third test, that the activity is not related to the exempt purpose of the organization, is the most subjective. Here are some examples of how this works:

1. A performing arts school can sell tickets to its student performances without paying tax. The student performances are related to the exempt purpose.
2. Sale of original paintings by an art museum has been seen as an NRB, but the rental of paintings was viewed as exempt.
3. Sale of sea science books by an aquarium was held to be exempt, but the sale of ashtrays and jewelry made from shells was NRB income.

It's not the end of the world if your activity is subject to NRB income tax. It merely results in increased expenses. But before deciding to pursue the project, get expert advice concerning its taxability. If it is taxable and you have not included this liability in your budget, you might find that a potentially profitable enterprise is not so worthwhile.

A far more serious threat is that the IRS could revoke your tax exemption for all of your activities based on the percentage of your total income that you receive from NRB. If this were to occur, all of your revenue, regardless of its source, would become taxable. And you would lose the ability to receive tax-deductible donations.

This happened to a social club that started investing in oil and gas drilling. Eventually the club's investments were so lucrative that it was receiving 70 percent of its income from the drilling. Another 20 percent came from interest income and 10 percent from membership fees. It lost its tax exemption.

The case doesn't need to be as extreme as the social club's to threaten your tax exemption. Generally, the IRS will allow an organization to devote 15 to 20 percent of its expenditures and efforts to an NRB before it questions the organization's tax exemption.

What can you do if your NRB is so successful that it threatens your tax exemption? Start a for-profit feeder business. Create a separate entity to conduct the NRB activity—a for-profit enterprise that donates its profits to your organization. There are many advantages to this separation. In addition to protecting your tax exempt status, for-profit enterprises

1. Are more attractive candidates for bank loans than nonprofits. Bankers understanding the profit-making world and are more likely to take a chance of loaning to a for-profit enterprise.
2. Reduce your business risk. If the NRB fails, it won't threaten your organization's existence.
3. Are eligible for assistance from the Small Business Administration. This can be a great resource.

NRB income ventures are a very attractive option for nonprofits. They expand you revenue possibilities far beyond the resources available through fund-raising and fees.

But they are very risky. Look before you leap.

BIBLIOGRAPHY

"Age Discrimination." *Ideas & Perspectives* (Independent School Management) 11, no. 13 (November 10, 1986):49–51.

Andresky, Jill. "Fire-Proof Executives?" *Forbes* 140, no. 8 (October 6, 1988):104–8.

Anthony, Robert N., and Regina E. Herzlinger. *Management Control in Nonprofit Organizations*. Homewood, IL: Richard D. Irwin, 1975.

Becker, Sarah, and Donna Glenn. *Off Your Duffs and Up Your Assets*. Rockville Center, NY: Farnsworth, 1985.

"Beware the Job Reference Hoax." *Executive Strategies* (Research Institute of America) (February 15, 1987):1–2.

Bittel, Lester R. *What Every Supervisor Should Know*, 5th edn. New York: McGraw-Hill, 1985.

Braswell, Ronald, Karen Fortin, and Jerome S. Osteryoung. *Financial Management for Not-for-Profit Organizations*. New York: John Wiley & Sons, 1984.

Brown, Frances C. "Shortage of Teachers Prompts Talent Hunt by Education Officials." *Wall Street Journal* 209, no. 10 (January 15, 1987):1, 15.

Bryce, Herrington J. *Financial and Strategic Management for Nonprofit Organizations*. Englewood Cliffs, NJ: Prentice-Hall, 1987.

Callahan, Raymond E. *Education and the Cult of Efficiency*. Chicago, IL: University of Chicago Press, 1962.

"Can Corporate Venturing Succeed?" *I.N.E. Reports* 2; no. 86 (August 1986):3.

Davis, Pamela. "Nonprofit Organizations and Liability Insurance." Los Angeles, CA: California Community Foundation, 1987.

Drucker, Peter F. *Management.* New York: Harper & Row, 1974.

————. *The Practice of Management.* London: Pan Books, 1979.

Durtin, Richard T. *Running Your Own Show.* New York: Mentor Executive Library, 1982.

Eden, Rick, David Lyons, Judith Payne, and Alan Bunk. *Indirect Costs,* Santa Monica, CA: Rand, 1986.

"Effective Internal Accounting Control for Nonprofit Organizations." New York: Price Waterhouse, 1982.

The Effective Nonprofit Executive Handbook. San Francisco, CA: Public Management Institute, 1982.

Firstenberg, Paul B. *Managing for Profit in the Nonprofit World.* New York: Foundation Center, 1986.

Galloway, Joseph M. *The Unrelated Business Income Tax.* New York: John Wiley and Sons, 1982.

Half, Robert. *How to Check References When References are Hard to Check.* Robert Half International, 1986.

Haller, Leon. *Financial Resource Management for Non-Profit Organizations.* Englewood Cliffs, NJ: Prentice-Hall, 1982.

Hopkins, Bruce R. *The Law of Tax-Exempt Organizations,* 5th edn. New York: John Wiley and Sons, 1987.

Kaye, Jude. "Reference Guide 1988." *NonProfit Times* 2, no. 1 (April 1988):44–49.

Kelly, James M. "Women, the Handicapped, and Older Employees." In *Handbook of Human Resources Administration,* 2nd edn., ed. Joseph J. Famularo, pp. 69/1–69/19. New York: McGraw-Hill, 1986.

Kelly, James M., and Lee S. Gassler. "Minorities." In *Handbook of Human Resources Administration,* 2d edn., ed. Joseph J. Famularo, pp. 68/1–68/30. New York: McGraw-Hill, 1986.

King, William R. "Strategic Planning in Nonprofit Organizations." New York: Amacom, 1979.

Kurtz, Daniel L. *Board Liability.* Mount Kisco, NY: Moyer Bell, 1968.

Kyd, Charles W. "Excuses, Excuses." *Inc.* 9, no. 9 (August 1987):87–88.

Lane, Mark J. *Legal Handbook for Nonprofit Organizations.* New York: Amacom, 1980.

Leftwich, Richard H., and Ansel M. Sharp. *Economics of Social Issues,* 4th edn. Dallas, TX: Business Publications, 1980.

Leonard, William T. "The Employment Interview." In *Handbook of Human Resources Administration,* 2nd edn., ed. Joseph J. Famularo, pp. 14/1–14/16. New York: McGraw-Hill, 1986.

Lewin, Tamar. "A Grueling Struggle for Equality." *New York Times,* November 9, 1986, pp. 12F–13F.

Lord, Richard. *$$ The Non-Profit Management Reports.* Cleveland, OH: Third Sector Press, 1987.

Lyons, Paul J. *Managing Contributed Funds & Assets.* Washington, D.C.: The Taft Group, 1985.

Milani, Ken. "Financial Management and Budgeting." In *The Nonprofit Organization Handbook,* 2nd edn., ed. Tracy Daniel Connors, pp. 47/1–47/21. New York: McGraw-Hill, 1988.

Morrell, Lou. "From Business Management to Chief Financial Officer." *NAIS Administrative Forum* (Fall 1986):7–11.

"Negligent Hiring Mounts as a Legal Threat to Employers." *Wall Street Journal,* December 23, 1986, p. 1.

Nelson, Stephen. "To Catch a Thief." *Inc.* 10, no. 1 (January 1988):89–90.

Nolan, John. *Management Audit.* Radnor, PA: Chilton Book Company, 1984.

Parisi, Rory. "Employee Terminations." In *Handbook of Human Resources Administration,* 2nd edn., ed. Joseph J. Famularo, pp. 64/1–64/16. New York: McGraw-Hill, 1986.

Pell, Arthur R. *Be a Better Employment Interviewer.* Huntington, NY: Personnel Publications, 1983.

Popell, Steven D. "Effectively Manage Receivables to Cut Costs." In *Growing Concerns,* ed. Harvard Business Review, pp. 199–206. New York: John Wiley & Sons, 1984.

Ricks, Thomas E. "Court Will Decide if AIDS Victims Enjoy Rights of the Handicapped." *Wall Street Journal,* November 5, 1986, p. 39.

Rollinson, Randy. "NonProfit Risk: Reward Venture Stream." *Nonprofit Marketing Insider* 11, no. 20 (September 30, 1986):2–3.

Romano, Patrick L. "Cash Management." In *The Accountant as Business Advisor,* ed. William K. Grollman. New York: Ronald Press, 1986.

Setterberg, Fred, and Kary Schulman. *Beyond Profit.* New York: Harper & Row, 1985.

Stancill, James McNeill. "Getting the Most From Your Banking Relationship." In *Growing Concerns,* ed. Harvard Business Review, pp. 234–42. New York: John Wiley & Sons, 1984.

Sterne, Larry. "Changes Proposed in UBIT Laws." *NonProfit Times* 1, no 10 (January 1988):3, 13.

"To Venture or Not to Venture." *I.N.E. Reports* 2, no. 86 (August 1986):2.

Treusch, Paul E., and Norman A. Sugarman. *Tax Exempt Charitable Organizations,* 2nd edn. Philadelphia, PA: American Law Institute, 1983.

Vinter, Robert D., and Rhea K. Kish. *Budgeting for Not-for-Profit Organizations.* New York: The Free Press, 1984.

Wacht, Richard F. *Financial Management in Nonprofit Organizations.* Atlanta, GA: Georgia State University, 1984.

INDEX

tax exempt status, loss of, 150–51
"time-value" of money, 25, 102
traditional budget, 83–85
transaction costs, 30, 32–34, 38
Treasury Bills (T–Bills), 35–36

unacceptable exposures, 55–60

variable costs, 91–92, 94

working capital, 99

ABOUT THE AUTHOR

RICHARD LORD drew upon 16 years of nonprofit management experience to devise the strategies presented in this book. He has specialized in developing administrative systems and applying the concepts of for-profit financial management to the nonprofit world. His career has included working with nonprofits in Europe and Latin America as well as in the United States. He has served on boards of directors and advisory boards of a variety of nonprofit service organizations. Lord received an M.A. from Boston University and completed postgraduate studies in finance at New York University's Graduate School of Business Administration. He is currently president of The Management Group, a consulting firm concentrating on nonprofits, which is based in New York City.